MICHAEL JACKSON

MICHAEL JACKSON

Lois P. Nicholson

CHELSEA HOUSE PUBLISHERS
New York   Philadelphia

Chelsea House Publishers
Editorial Director Richard Rennert
Executive Managing Editor Karyn Gullen Browne
Copy Chief Robin James
Picture Editor Adrian G. Allen
Art Director Robert Mitchell
Manufacturing Director Gerald Levine

Black Americans of Achievement
Senior Editor Sean Dolan

Staff for MICHAEL JACKSON
Editorial Assistant Annie McDonnell
Assistant Designer John Infantino
Picture Researcher Lisa Kirchner
Cover Illustrator Bradford Brown

3 5 7 9 8 6 4 2

Library of Congress Cataloging-in-Publication Data
Nicholson, Lois P.
  Michael Jackson / Lois P. Nicholson.
    p. cm.—(Black Americans of achievement)
  Includes bibliographical references and index.
  ISBN   0-7910-1929-2.
          0-7910-1930-6 (pbk.)
    1. Jackson, Michael, 1958– —Juvenile literature. 2. Rock mu-
sicians—United States—Biography—Juvenile literature. [1. Jack-
son, Michael, 1958– . 2. Entertainers. 3. Afro-Americans—Biog-
raphy.] I. Title. II. Series.
ML3930.J25N5 1994   93-39777
782.42166'092—dc20   CIP
[B]   AC MN

*Frontispiece: Michael Jackson first
captured the attention of the American
public as the 10-year-old lead singer of
the Jackson Five. In little more than a
decade, he became the most popular
entertainer in the world.*

CONTENTS

BLACK AMERICANS OF ACHIEVEMENT

HENRY AARON
baseball great

KAREEM ABDUL-JABBAR
basketball great

RALPH ABERNATHY
civil rights leader

ALVIN AILEY
choreographer

MUHAMMAD ALI
heavyweight champion

RICHARD ALLEN
*religious leader and
social activist*

MAYA ANGELOU
author

LOUIS ARMSTRONG
musician

ARTHUR ASHE
tennis great

JOSEPHINE BAKER
entertainer

JAMES BALDWIN
author

BENJAMIN BANNEKER
scientist and mathematician

AMIRI BARAKA
poet and playwright

COUNT BASIE
bandleader and composer

ROMARE BEARDEN
artist

JAMES BECKWOURTH
frontiersman

MARY MCLEOD BETHUNE
educator

JULIAN BOND
civil rights leader and politician

GWENDOLYN BROOKS
poet

JIM BROWN
football great

RALPH BUNCHE
diplomat

STOKELY CARMICHAEL
civil rights leader

GEORGE WASHINGTON
CARVER
botanist

RAY CHARLES
musician

CHARLES CHESNUTT
author

JOHN COLTRANE
musician

BILL COSBY
entertainer

PAUL CUFFE
merchant and abolitionist

COUNTEE CULLEN
poet

BENJAMIN DAVIS, SR., AND
BENJAMIN DAVIS, JR.
military leaders

SAMMY DAVIS, JR.
entertainer

FATHER DIVINE
religious leader

FREDERICK DOUGLASS
abolitionist editor

CHARLES DREW
physician

W. E. B. DU BOIS
scholar and activist

PAUL LAURENCE DUNBAR
poet

KATHERINE DUNHAM
dancer and choreographer

DUKE ELLINGTON
bandleader and composer

RALPH ELLISON
author

JULIUS ERVING
basketball great

JAMES FARMER
civil rights leader

ELLA FITZGERALD
singer

MARCUS GARVEY
black nationalist leader

JOSH GIBSON
baseball great

DIZZY GILLESPIE
musician

WHOOPI GOLDBERG
entertainer

ALEX HALEY
author

PRINCE HALL
social reformer

MATTHEW HENSON
explorer

CHESTER HIMES
author

BILLIE HOLIDAY
singer

LENA HORNE
entertainer

LANGSTON HUGHES
poet

ZORA NEALE HURSTON
author

JESSE JACKSON
civil rights leader and politician

MICHAEL JACKSON
entertainer

JACK JOHNSON
heavyweight champion

JAMES WELDON JOHNSON
author

MAGIC JOHNSON
basketball great

SCOTT JOPLIN
composer

BARBARA JORDAN
politician

MICHAEL JORDAN
basketball great

CORETTA SCOTT KING
civil rights leader

MARTIN LUTHER KING, JR.
civil rights leader

LEWIS LATIMER
scientist

SPIKE LEE
filmmaker

CARL LEWIS
champion athlete

JOE LOUIS
heavyweight champion

RONALD MCNAIR
astronaut

MALCOLM X
militant black leader

THURGOOD MARSHALL
Supreme Court justice

TONI MORRISON
author

ELIJAH MUHAMMAD
religious leader

EDDIE MURPHY
entertainer

JESSE OWENS
champion athlete

SATCHEL PAIGE
baseball great

CHARLIE PARKER
musician

GORDON PARKS
photographer

ROSA PARKS
civil rights leader

SIDNEY POITIER
actor

ADAM CLAYTON
POWELL, JR.
political leader

COLIN POWELL
military leader

LEONTYNE PRICE
opera singer

A. PHILIP RANDOLPH
labor leader

PAUL ROBESON
singer and actor

JACKIE ROBINSON
baseball great

DIANA ROSS
entertainer

BILL RUSSELL
basketball great

JOHN RUSSWURM
publisher

SOJOURNER TRUTH
antislavery activist

HARRIET TUBMAN
antislavery activist

NAT TURNER
slave revolt leader

DENMARK VESEY
slave revolt leader

ALICE WALKER
author

MADAM C. J. WALKER
entrepreneur

BOOKER T. WASHINGTON
educator and racial spokesman

IDA WELLS-BARNETT
civil rights leader

WALTER WHITE
civil rights leader

OPRAH WINFREY
entertainer

STEVIE WONDER
musician

RICHARD WRIGHT
author

ON
ACHIEVEMENT

Coretta Scott King

BEFORE YOU BEGIN this book, I hope you will ask yourself what the word *excellence* means to you. I think that it's a question we should all ask, and keep asking as we grow older and change. Because the truest answer to it should never change. When you think of excellence, perhaps you think of success at work; or of becoming wealthy; or meeting the right person, getting married, and having a good family life.

Those important goals are worth striving for, but there is a better way to look at excellence. As Martin Luther King, Jr., said in one of his last sermons, "I want you to be first in love. I want you to be first in moral excellence. I want you to be first in generosity. If you want to be important, wonderful. If you want to be great, wonderful. But recognize that he who is greatest among you shall be your servant."

My husband, Martin Luther King, Jr., knew that the true meaning of achievement is service. When I met him, in 1952, he was already ordained as a Baptist preacher and was working toward a doctoral degree at Boston University. I was studying at the New England Conservatory and dreamed of accomplishments in music. We married a year later, and after I graduated the following year we moved to Montgomery, Alabama. We didn't know it then, but our notions of achievement were about to undergo a dramatic change.

You may have read or heard about what happened next. What began with the boycott of a local bus line grew into a national movement, and by the time he was assassinated in 1968 my husband had fashioned a black movement powerful enough to shatter forever the practice of racial segregation. What you may not have read about is where he got his method for resisting injustice without compromising his religious beliefs.

He adopted the strategy of nonviolence from a man of a different race, who lived in a different country, and even practiced a different religion. The man was Mahatma Gandhi, the great leader of India, who devoted his life to serving humanity in the spirit of love and nonviolence. It was in these principles that Martin discovered his method for social reform. More than anything else, those two principles were the key to his achievements.

This book is about black Americans who served society through the excellence of their achievements. It forms a part of the rich history of black men and women in America—a history of stunning accomplishments in every field of human endeavor, from literature and art to science, industry, education, diplomacy, athletics, jurisprudence, even polar exploration.

Not all of the people in this history had the same ideals, but I think you will find something that all of them had in common. Like Martin Luther King, Jr., they all decided to become "drum majors" and serve humanity. In that principle—whether it was expressed in books, inventions, or song—they found something outside themselves to use as a goal and a guide. Something that showed them a way to serve others, instead of only living for themselves.

Reading the stories of these courageous men and women not only helps us discover the principles that we will use to guide our own lives but also teaches us about our black heritage and about America itself. It is crucial for us to know the heroes and heroines of our history and to realize that the price we paid in our struggle for equality in America was dear. But we must also understand that we have gotten as far as we have partly because America's democratic system and ideals made it possible.

We are still struggling with racism and prejudice. But the great men and women in this series are a tribute to the spirit of our democratic ideals and the system in which they have flourished. And that makes their stories special and worth knowing. ❦

1

CREATING MAGIC

❧

O N THE NIGHT of May 16, 1983, almost 50 million people watched one of the most spectacular performances ever seen on television. But if Michael Jackson had been in charge, the event never would have happened.

The occasion was the special "Motown 25," a televised tribute to Motown Records' 25 years of producing hit records by black entertainers. Started in Detroit, Michigan, in 1959 by Berry Gordy, Motown became the first black-owned record company to challenge successfully the giant New York–based recording empires. The lineup of stars who had been developed there and who would appear on the television special included Diana Ross and the Supremes, the Temptations, Stevie Wonder, Smokey Robinson—and the Jackson Five.

The Jackson Five—brothers among the nine children of a Gary, Indiana, steel worker and musician—had signed with Motown when Michael Jackson was 10 years old. Under Gordy's careful direction, the group's recordings had shot to the top of the charts, while their concert tours broke box-office records around the world.

It had been six years since the Jacksons had left Motown Records, although some of the individual brothers continued to record for Gordy's label, and

Even at the height of his popularity, Jackson maintained a deep respect for the pioneers of black popular music. Here, he is pictured with Chuck Berry, one of the first rock-and-roll stars.

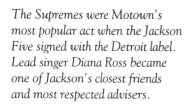

The Supremes were Motown's most popular act when the Jackson Five signed with the Detroit label. Lead singer Diana Ross became one of Jackson's closest friends and most respected advisers.

Michael had recently begun his own solo career. He had also developed his own dancing style, taking break dancing to new levels. The family's departure from Motown had also led to a bitter legal battle over their contract.

So when the producers of "Motown 25" asked Michael Jackson to do a musical number with his brothers and a solo on the show, he at first said no. He was grateful to Motown for giving his family its start in show business, but that was in the past; the family and the record company had parted ways years earlier. Besides, Michael did not like performing on television.

It took a personal visit from Berry Gordy to persuade Michael to change his mind. He agreed to do some of the Jacksons' old songs with his brothers and a solo of his recent hit song, "Billie Jean," on the program.

Although, at age 24, he was the youngest of the brothers, Michael took charge of their rehearsals. Always a perfectionist, he drove himself and his brothers hard during the rehearsals at his home in California. He worked them on their vocal and dance routines with so much intensity that he put little time into planning his own number. He had no time for the animals in his private zoo behind the house: the llama and fawns, the ram and boa constrictor, the swans and peacocks and parrots. The room filled with video games remained silent. The hundreds of old musicals and Walt Disney movies in his video collection went unwatched.

The show was scheduled to be taped before a live audience about a month before it would be seen on television. But days before the taping, Jackson still had not worked out his own solo. He knew only that he wanted to wear a dark, sinister-looking hat that would give him the appearance of a spy or a gangster.

The night before the taping, Jackson sat alone in his kitchen. The popcorn and ice cream machines did not tempt him. He stood in the middle of the room with the spy hat in his hands and listened to "Billie Jean." He played it again, turning up the volume so loud that it rattled the dishes, letting the beat and the song saturate him. His hands and feet began to move, as if they were ordering him about, instead of him telling his body what to do.

Jackson was determined to create magic whenever he performed—"to put something together that's so unusual, so unexpected, that it blows people's heads off," he explained. "Something ahead of the times. Five steps ahead of what people are thinking. . . . When I hit the stage it's all of a sudden a magic from somewhere that comes and the spirit just hits you, and you lose control of yourself."

Michael had picked up a break-dance step from watching kids dancing on street corners. He had embellished it—combining it with some other steps of his own—and enjoyed practicing it privately. Jackson's dance resembled the Moonwalk, which kids were already doing on the street. Dancing his version of the Moonwalk, Michael seemed to be walking backward

With hits like "Tears of a Clown" and "My Girl," Smokey Robinson and the Miracles were early role models for the Jackson Five. Michael and his brothers learned to choreograph their own shows by watching groups like the Miracles and the Temptations perform.

and forward at the same time, just like a robot or someone walking on the moon. He loved doing the dance in private, but he had never performed it before an audience. Now, in his kitchen in the middle of the night, the rhythm of "Billie Jean" shaking the room and impelling his body, he decided to do the Moonwalk for the first time in public, on the "Motown 25" show.

Jackson did not tell anybody about his plans. The next day, as the taping ran hours late, he stole away from his brothers and continued to practice secretly. Finally, the young men's turn came, and the Jackson Five did their medley of old favorites to enthusiastic applause. Then the lights went out, except for a spotlight on Michael, who was wearing a glittery black jacket and his trademark single white glove. He walked to the side of the stage by the curtains while his brothers left the stage in the darkness.

"I'd like to say those were the good old days," Jackson said to the audience. "Those were magic moments with all my brothers . . ." Meanwhile, he reached behind his back as a stagehand placed the hat into his hand unseen. "But what I really like are the newer songs." With that, the opening drumbeat of "Billie Jean" broke over the crowd, which reacted with cheers and screams of recognition.

From that opening beat until the end of the song, Michael's concentration was so intense that he completely forgot about the audience. When he opened his eyes again, he saw a mass of people standing and applauding what *Rolling Stone* magazine called "the most electrifying five minutes of the evening."

Jackson had accomplished his goal; he had created magic. His brothers watched in amazement from the wings. It was their first opportunity to see how Michael had developed since he had left the band. His parents and sisters were among the cheering audience. Backstage, his family mobbed him with hugs and kisses, while other performers showered him with congratulations.

Although Jackson recognized this as one of the happiest moments of his life, he also felt disappointed. Able to spin like an ice skater without ice or skates, he had planned to perform a long spin and then freeze, suspended on one toe. But he had been unable to hold the pose for as long as he intended.

"The performance was still gnawing at me," Jackson wrote in *Moonwalk,* "and I wasn't satisfied until a little boy looked up at me with stars in his eyes . . . and said, 'Man, who taught you to dance like that?' . . . For the first time that evening I really felt good about what I had accomplished that night. I said to myself, I must have done really well because children are honest."

The next day, one of Jackson's heroes, dancer Fred Astaire, called him. "You're a hell of a mover," Astaire told Michael. "Man, you really put them on their asses last night."

The compliment, coming from a man whom Jackson and many others considered the greatest dancer of them all, was all the reward Michael wanted. Later, he visited Astaire and demonstrated the Moonwalk and other steps for the aging star. Dancers Gene Kelly and Sammy Davis, Jr., also praised Michael's performance.

Millions of viewers of the "Motown 25" show "discovered" Jackson that night. Most people responded as if they had never seen him perform before, or only dimly remembered the cute, six-year-old lead singer of the Jackson Five. Many regarded him as an overnight sensation, one of those rare performers who wake up one morning to discover that they have suddenly become superstars. But Michael Jackson had changed the world of music and dancing long before that night. ❦

2

BORN TO DANCE

$\mathbf{M}$ICHAEL JOE JACKSON, the seventh child of Joe and Katherine Jackson, was born on a late summer night in Gary, Indiana, on August 29, 1958. A grim industrial city standing on the northern tip of Indiana near Chicago, Illinois, Gary, with its growing inner-city decay, shared the plight of many of America's urban centers. Dotted with old factories and plagued by unemployment, the city was made up of streets lined with rows of small, single-family dwellings. At night, smokestacks lit the sky over Gary with a fiery luminous blush, illuminating the city's tough working-class character.

The nature of Gary was best revealed in its teeming street life. Known to many as Sin City in the 1960s, the town was a mecca for people from Chicago as well as other parts of Indiana who wished to escape the watchful eyes of family and friends. Joe and Katherine Jackson lived at 825 Jackson Street, right in the middle of the Sin City environment. Raising a family in those surroundings posed many challenges for Michael's parents. One of the biggest

In the 1960s, Gary, Indiana, was a grim industrial city, its streets lined with abandoned factories and unemployed workers.

challenges was keeping the family fed and clothed on the meager income that Joe earned as a crane operator for U.S. Steel. Katherine supplemented the family's earnings as a part-time employee at Sears, Roebuck and Company.

Married in 1949, Joseph Jackson and the former Katherine Scruse were typical of many young couples of the era. At age 21, Joe represented the strong, determined provider, while 18-year-old Katherine filled the role of the supportive, nurturing wife and mother. Both attractive individuals, the two formed a handsome couple.

Joe Jackson was born in Arkansas and raised in Tennessee. The son of a stern Lutheran father, he brought his own childhood experience to rearing his own family. "My father was very strict," recalled Joe. "He was a schoolteacher and he treated us just like the rest of the kids in school. I'm glad that happened. I might not have been able to do the things I've done without a very strict raising."

From his strict Tennessee upbringing, Joe learned that survival often depended on hard work and discipline. As an adult, he believed that these principles were also essential in raising a family in urban Gary in the 1960s.

Complementing Joe's stern, assertive nature, Katherine brought a quiet, calming quality to the family. A beautiful woman with striking eyes, Katherine grew up in Alabama, where she demonstrated an early love for music. She played the clarinet and the piano. When she was a child, she developed polio, and the disease left her with a slight limp. Missing a great deal of time from school, Katherine felt fortunate to survive the dreaded disease that took the lives of so many other children. Unable to perform in front of others, she was later delighted to teach her daughters to play her favorite instruments.

Katherine possessed a strong faith in the teachings of the Jehovah's Witnesses, and her beliefs strongly influenced the family's values. The children would later accompany her to Kingdom Hall, the denomination's traditional place of worship, but her husband did not.

Joe and Katherine's first child, Maureen, was born in 1950. Jackie, Tito, Jermaine, LaToya, Marlon, Michael, Randy, and Janet followed. Katherine and Joe reared their large family in an extremely small one-story dwelling. "Our family's house in Gary was tiny, only three rooms really, but at the time it seemed much larger to me," recalled Michael. "When we went back to Gary years later, we were all surprised at how tiny that house was. I had remembered it as being large, but you could take five steps from the front door and you'd be out the back. It was no bigger than a garage, but when we lived there it seemed fine to us kids."

Michael's earliest childhood memories were of two loving parents who worked hard and instilled strong values in their large family. Recalling his mother's influence, Michael wrote, "We never had to look for anyone else with my mother around. The lessons she taught us were invaluable. Kindness, love, and consideration for other people headed her list. Don't hurt people. Never beg. Never freeload. Those were sins at our house. She always wanted us to give, but she never wanted us to ask or beg. That's the way she is."

Michael loved to tell stories about his mother's kindness and generosity. One of his favorites involved a strange man who came to the Jacksons' door one day. "He was bleeding so badly you could see where he'd been around the neighborhood," Michael remembered. "No one would let him in. Finally he got to our door and he started banging and knocking. Mother let him in at once."

Although Michael and Joe Jackson would have many bitter disagreements in later years, Michael's earliest recollections of his father were fond ones. "The earliest memories I have of my father," Michael later wrote, "are of him coming home from the steel mill with a big bag of glazed doughnuts for all of us. My brothers and I could really eat back then and that bag would disappear with a snap of the fingers."

According to Michael, Joe's work at the steel plant was "tough, mind-numbing work." As far back as Michael could remember, music was always a part of the Jackson household. It provided a diversion for both Joe and Katherine. Joe and his brother were part of a group called the Falcons, a local rhythm-and-blues band in which the two men played guitar. Their music, mostly early rock-and-roll and blues standards, included works by Chuck Berry, Little Richard, and Otis Redding, among others. "All those styles were amazing," Michael later observed, "and each had an influence on us, although we were too young to know it at the time."

Practicing in the Jackson family's living room in Gary, the combined children from the families of the band members created a large group. "Music was what we did for entertainment and those times helped keep us together and kind of encouraged my father to be a family-oriented man," remembered Michael. "The Jackson Five were born out of this tradition."

Seeking other ways to keep her growing brood off the streets, Katherine provided additional entertainment for the family at home. There were card games and other indoor games such as Scrabble and Monopoly. When the Falcons were

The seventh of nine children, Michael was a shy, insecure child. Each week, he spent his allowance on candy that he gave to the other schoolchildren in exchange for their friendship.

not practicing, the Jackson family made its own music. Katherine led the family with her lovely soprano voice, with Joe accompanying on his prized electric guitar. Together, they sang traditional songs such as "Cotton Fields" and "You Are My Sunshine." From the beginning, Joe and Katherine were amazed by how well their children could sing.

During this period, the Jacksons' eldest daughter Maureen got married and moved to Kentucky with her husband, Nathaniel Brown. The two other daughters, LaToya Yvonne and Janet Dameta, were no problem, but Joe and Katherine worried about their sons growing up in such a tough, gang-dominated neighborhood. Sigmund Esco, who was also called Jackie, showed promise as an athlete, demonstrating great skill in both baseball and basketball with his tall, solid build. Tariano Adaryl, or Tito, was a quiet young man, who strongly resembled his father. Jermaine La Jaune possessed a slow, easy smile that made him a hit with all the neighborhood girls, and Marlon David loved to dance, always showing off the latest steps at parties. Michael Joe showed an early love for animals and a spirited, happy personality, while Steven Randall, or Randy, was happy to follow along behind his older brothers, especially Michael.

According to Katherine Jackson, the children never got into any serious trouble and rarely needed to be disciplined. "After you instill in the two oldest what they can and cannot do, the others automatically follow," she said. But from the start she noticed something different about Michael. "You know how babies move uncoordinated?" she recalled. "He never moved that way. When he danced, it was like he was an older person."

There was, however, one temptation that the musical brothers could not resist. The Falcons continued to enjoy limited success as a local musical group, playing in Gary, neighboring Chicago, and in clubs and colleges. Joe was able to earn a little extra money for the family while playing rhythm and blues on his pride and joy, his electric guitar. "The closet where the guitar was kept was considered an almost sacred place," Michael later recalled. "Needless to say, it was off limits to us kids." When the band practiced, Tito, Jackie, and Jermaine observed every move their father made on his guitar.

Having played the saxophone in high school, Tito displayed a special interest in his father's instrument. "He could tell his hands were big enough to grab the chords and slip the riffs that my father played," remembered Michael. "It made sense that he'd catch on because Tito looked so much like my father that we all expected him to share Dad's talents."

But Tito also knew the rule that his father had laid down about his prized guitar: no one was to touch the instrument when Joe Jackson was not at home. "Jackie, Tito, and Jermaine were careful to see that Mom was in the kitchen when they 'borrowed' the guitar," Michael later admitted. Careful not to make any sounds while using it, the boys regularly removed the guitar from its hiding place, smuggling it into their bedroom without a sound. The trio took turns practicing scales or playing along with whatever song was on the radio or record player. "They'd try to figure out how to get the 'Green Onions' part they'd hear on the radio," Michael recalled.

Occasionally, four-year-old Michael was allowed to sneak in and watch his older brothers "jamming." Katherine once discovered her sons in their crime,

For the first eight years of his life, Michael lived crowded together with his brothers and sisters in this modest house on Jackson Street in Gary.

but she vowed not to tell their father if they promised to be cautious. She considered it a small price to pay to keep her sons out of the gangs and away from the evils of the streets lurking just outside their door.

But it was only a matter of time before Joe Jackson discovered his sons' secret. After breaking a string one day, the brothers panicked. With no time to have the string repaired, they simply returned the guitar to the closet and hoped their father would believe the string broke on its own accord. When he discovered the broken string, Joe Jackson was furious. Hearing Tito crying, Michael went to his brother's room. Looking stern and angry, Michael's father was holding his prized guitar above the bed where the frightened Tito was lying. But Joe Jackson did not wait for an explanation. "He gave Tito a hard penetrating look," Michael later remembered, "and said, 'Let me see what you can do.'"

Regaining his composure, Tito played a few runs that he had taught himself. Joe immediately recognized Tito's talents and realized that his son had been practicing seriously on the guitar, not just fooling around. When Tito, Jackie, and Jermaine played and sang together, their father was amazed at how good they were. Soon, the three brothers were woodshedding, or rehearsing, together regularly under their father's guidance. "We'd just woodshed together and he'd give us tips and teach us techniques on the guitar," said Michael. As Joe Jackson came to understand the potential his sons possessed, he began to spend more time with the boys and less time with the Falcons.

When Joe Jackson failed to come home from work one day at the usual hour, Katherine became increasingly worried. As the hours passed, Katherine's worries turned to anger, and she was ready to scold her husband for worrying her and the boys by staying out so late. When Joe finally came through the door, however, Katherine could see the mischievous smile on her husband's face and immediately felt relieved. Joe was hiding something behind his back. It was a new gleaming red guitar that he had bought for Tito and anyone else in the family who was willing to practice.

Joe continued to provide equipment for the group. "Jermaine got a bass and an amp," recalled Michael. "There were shakers for Jackie. Our bedroom and living room began to look like a music store." While Tito and Jackie played guitar, Jermaine, who had the finest voice, sang and played bass. Maureen and LaToya provided accompaniment on violin and clarinet, as the younger children watched and listened. Always an attentive observer, Michael displayed a special interest in the activities of his older siblings. "We had become a real band," Michael later remembered proudly. "I was like a sponge, watching everyone, and trying to learn everything I could. I was most fascinated when watching Jermaine because he was the singer at the time and he was a big brother to me—Marlon was too close to me in age for that. It was Jermaine who would walk me

Soul singer Sam Cooke was one of the many performers whose style Michael copied during his early days in the Jackson Five. "I was like a sponge," Jackson later recalled, "watching everyone, and trying to learn everything I could."

to kindergarten and whose clothes would be handed down to me. When he did something, I tried to imitate him. When I was successful at it, my brothers and Dad would laugh, but when I began singing, they listened."

"I was singing in a baby voice then and just imitating sounds," said Michael, remembering how young he was at the time. "I was so young I didn't know what many of the words meant, but the more I sang, the better I got."

Katherine Jackson was grateful that her children were engaged in a family activity, but Michael's mother also had reservations about her husband's plans for the family. The purchase of musical instruments required money needed for food and clothing. Joe Jackson was convinced that all the sacrifices would eventually produce results, and Katherine realized that it was useless to attempt to stifle his enthusiasm. While the children slept at night, Joe shared his hopes, dreams, and plans with his wife. "Sometimes I'd hear Mom and Dad fight when the subject of money was brought up," recalled Michael, "because all those instruments meant having to go without a little something we needed each week. Dad was persuasive, though, and he didn't miss a trick."

Joe often visited local dances and night spots, observing musical groups. He noted everything about the songs, style, moves, and costumes of the most successful performers. Seeing that other groups had drummers and organists, Joe recruited two boys for the group, Johnny Jackson and Ronnie Rancifer. Teaching the kids what he learned from the other groups, Joe demanded that the children practice for hours every day. As time passed, the members of the group changed. Maureen and LaToya eventually dropped out, as did Ronnie. Marlon and Michael replaced them.

Recalling those early years, Joe Jackson told an interviewer, "I rehearsed them about three years before I turned them loose. That is practically every day for at least two or three hours. When the other kids would be out on the street playing games, my boys were in the house working, trying to learn how to be something in life. They got a little upset about the whole thing in the beginning because the other kids were out there having a good time."

At the age of five, Michael could already sing just like his older brother Jermaine. When Joe Jackson discovered that the youngster could also play bongo drums while he sang, he made Michael a part of the group. Almost immediately, Michael became the lead singer—to the delight of all his brothers. "Michael was so energetic that at five years old he was like a leader," Jackie later remembered, "We saw that. . . . The speed was the thing. He would see somebody do something and he could do it right away."

Michael's gifts as a mimic proved invaluable to the group. Many of their early performances were based upon imitating the sounds and moves of many popular groups. "It was sort of frightening," Katherine Jackson later recalled. "He was so young. He didn't go out and play much. So, if you want me to tell you the truth, I don't know where he got it. He just knew."

"What I got from my father wasn't necessarily God-given, though the Bible says you reap what you sow," wrote Michael. "When we were coming along, Dad said that in a different way, but the message was just as clear: you could have all the talent in the world, but if you didn't prepare and plan, it wouldn't do you any good." Joe Jackson agreed. "I noticed that they were getting better and better," he remembered proudly. "Then I saw that after they became better, they enjoyed it more."

"We even had microphones in the house," recalled Michael. "They seemed like a real luxury at the time, especially to a woman who was trying to stretch a very small budget, but I've come to realize that having those microphones in our house wasn't just an attempt to keep up with the Joneses or anyone else in amateur night competitions. They were to help us prepare. I saw people at talent shows, who probably sounded great at home, clam up the moment they got in front of a microphone. Others started screaming their songs like they wanted to prove they didn't need the mikes. They didn't have the advantage that we did—an advantage that only experience can give you."

Dancing was as important as singing for many black musical groups of the 1960s. Many of the Motown groups used elaborate routines to accompany their songs, each song requiring different choreography. Michael idolized James Brown and became irritated when the television cameramen did not focus on James Brown's feet long enough for him to pick up his moves. "I always knew how to dance. I would watch Marlon's moves because Jermaine had the bass to carry, but also because I could keep up with Marlon, who was only a year older than me," recalled Michael. "Through our rehearsals, we were all becoming aware of our particular strengths and weaknesses as members of the group and the shift in responsibilities was happening naturally."

Michael was only five during the Jackson Five's first year, and he admits not remembering much about many aspects of it. "Most people have the luxury of careers that start when they're old enough to know exactly what they're doing and why, but, of course, that wasn't true of me," he later admitted. "When you're a show business child, you really don't have the maturity to understand a great deal of what is going on around you. People make a lot of decisions concerning your life when you're out of the room."

What Michael does remember is the music and the work. "I remember singing at the top of my voice and dancing with real joy and working too hard for a child," he told one reporter. In the years that followed, Joe Jackson continued to demand excellence from his sons; he wanted them to be the best. He had no idea just how good they would become. ❧

3

ALL WORK AND NO PLAY

IN 1964, MOST six-year-old American children were in first grade and spent most of their time playing and participating in other childhood activities. Michael Jackson entered first grade that year. Outside of school, however, his life bore little resemblance to that of other American children. Determined to mold his boys into a successful musical act, Joe Jackson continued to be a tough taskmaster. Recalling those days, he said, "When I say they liked it, I helped them when it got hard for them and when they felt disgusted as kids sometimes do . . . when they find it more work than they thought. You have to encourage them to get over that hump."

"We always rehearsed," recalled Michael. "Sometimes, late at night, we'd have time to play games or play with our toys. There might be a game of hide-and-go-seek or we'd jump rope, but that was about it. The majority of our time was spent working. I clearly remember running into the house with my brothers when my father came home, because we'd be in big trouble if we weren't ready to start rehearsals on time."

At night, Gary, Indiana, became a center of music and entertainment. People would come from as far away as Chicago to hear popular bands perform in Sin City's many bars and late-night clubs.

Perhaps no other entertainer had a greater impact on Jackson's stage presence than James Brown, pictured here with his band, the Famous Flames. Known as the Godfather of Soul, Brown's gospel-inspired swirling and sliding set a new standard for live performance among black entertainers.

The neighborhood children teased the Jackson brothers because the boys were always rehearsing and never had time to play. As the brothers practiced, they could hear the roar of the crowd at a nearby baseball park. In 1977, Michael told a reporter for the *Los Angeles Times*, "It's kind of a shame we didn't grow up doing what other kids did."

"We had to rehearse everyday after school when the other kids played," recalled Tito. "Our parents did push us, but it wasn't against our will. We loved music, it was a thrill to be making music at that age that sounded good and that adults seemed to like."

School provided a pleasant diversion for Michael. He loved his teachers and brought them gifts from his mother's jewelry box—until Katherine caught on to the source of Michael's presents. During the first grade, Michael participated in a school program in which he sang "Climb Every Mountain" from *The Sound of Music*. The audience rewarded Michael's spirited performance with an enthusiastic ovation. It was the first time that he had experienced the response of a live audience. "I had made them all happy," he recalled. "It was such a great feeling. I felt a little confused too, because I didn't think I had done anything special. I was just singing the way I sang at home every night."

Finally, in 1965, Joe Jackson felt his sons were ready to perform in public. Music was important in Gary, and the town's nightclubs and radio stations were always seeking quality acts. Joe had continued to visit clubs in Gary and Chicago on Saturday nights to catch the latest entertainers. Acting as a scout, he reported to his sons on what he had seen, what clothes the great acts were wearing, and the latest choreographic moves as well. Arriving home late on a Sunday evening, Joe often had to wait until the children returned from Kingdom Hall before he could share his exciting observations. "He'd assure me I could dance on one leg like James Brown if I'd only try this step," Michael said. "There I'd be, fresh out of church, and back in show business."

The Jacksons began to enter local contests when Michael was only six. Standing second from the left and facing the audience, Jermaine stood next to Michael, Jackie was on Jermaine's right, Tito on guitar took stage right, and Marlon was positioned next to him. The arrangement worked well, and with each performance, the group became more polished. Continually striving to surprise and delight their audiences, the family routinely changed and expanded their act, providing the Jacksons with constant new challenges.

"These talent shows, where a ten-minute, two-song set took as much energy as a ninety-minute concert, were our professional education," wrote Michael years later. Often driving long distances to reach their destinations, the Jackson brothers competed against all types of acts: comedians, drill teams, and other singing groups like themselves. But wherever they went, the Jacksons were always prepared. Joe Jackson carefully planned every last detail of their performance—clothes, shoes, hair, choreography—everything that would make an impression on a judge or an audience.

Joe continued to drive his sons at a relentless pace. He told them how James Brown sometimes fined the members of his group, the Famous Flames, for hitting a wrong note or making a misstep in their dance routine. Joe insisted that the boys always strive to be perfect. As the group's lead singer, Michael felt acute pressure. "I can remember being on stage at night after being sick in bed all day. It was hard to concentrate at those times, yet I knew all the things my brothers and I had to do so well that I could have performed all the routines in my sleep."

When Michael was eight, the Jacksons won the citywide talent show with their rendition of the Temptations' song "My Girl." The audience at Roosevelt High School went wild as Marlon and Jackie spun in unison like tops, using dance moves they had practiced endlessly. Jermaine and Michael alternated on the vocals. Singing lead, Michael's voice was high like a child's. But he possessed the vocal control of an adult, and he moved about the stage as if he owned it. Ecstatic over the victory, the family drove home with the trophy on the front seat. For once, Joe Jackson could not conceal his pride. "When you do it like you did tonight they can't not give it to you," he told the boys. Entering two other talent contests, the Jackson Five walked away with two first-place prizes. Soon, Joe was booking the Jacksons at shopping centers, benefits, and dances.

In 1967, American musical trends were rapidly changing. The invasion of English rock groups had created new interests, but more traditional groups such as Smokey Robinson and the Miracles, the Temptations, and the Impressions with Curtis Mayfield continued to draw large followings. Known as crossover groups, these established performers attracted both black and white fans. With their stylish sharkskin suits, expensive shoes, and slick hairstyles, they appeared in places such as Chicago's South Side, but they also drew white audiences in New York's Copacabana. This was the type of success that Joe Jackson wanted for his sons. Always looking to the future, he sought to combine a slicker, more modern look with standard rhythm and blues.

Michael maintained a rigorous schedule of school, rehearsals, and late-night performances. Arriving home at three or four o'clock in the morning, the children would be off to school at eight o'clock. Strategically planning the group's every move, Joe next signed the Jacksons to Steeltown, a Gary-based record label that produced the family's first single, "I'm a Big Boy Now." A standard rhythm-and-blues ballad reflecting the mid-1960s, the song featured a call-and-response vocal style between Michael and his brothers. Picked up for distribution, "Big Boy" achieved only limited success, but the subsequent airplay the record received resulted in the group's landing an important gig at a local club called Mr. Lucky's.

The Jackson Five played five shows per night at Mr. Lucky's, six nights a week, and earned from $5 to $8 a night. The boys always managed to take home

Though the Jackson Five were best known for their dance numbers, Michael also loved ballads, such as rhythm-and-blues singer Jackie Wilson's "Lonely Teardrops." From Wilson, Jackson would learn the sweet vocal style that he would use on many of his own hits.

some extra cash in their bulging pockets. As the audiences tossed money upon the stage, Michael learned to use dance steps to retrieve the cash. Dipping, spinning, and performing intricate splits, Michael grabbed the change as fast as the members of the audience could throw it. "I remember my pockets being so full of money that I couldn't keep my pants up," he said. Michael spent much of his $20 weekly allowance on candy, most of which he would give to other neighborhood children in order to keep their friendship.

A devoutly religious woman, Katherine Jackson disapproved of her sons performing in nightclubs, but the family sorely needed the extra money that the boys were making at the clubs. If she had known what her sons were being exposed to at these clubs, she undoubtedly would have been less understanding. "We worked in more than one club that had strippers in those days," Michael recalled years later. "I used to stand and watch a lady whose name was Mary Rose. I must have been nine or ten. The girl would take off her clothes and her panties and throw them to the audience. . . . My brothers and I would be watching all this, taking it in, and my father wouldn't mind. We were exposed to a lot doing that kind of circuit."

It was a routine practice among the male acts at the clubs to drill holes through the walls of ladies' dressing rooms and bathrooms. "Of course, I'm sure that my brothers and I were fighting over who got to look through the hole," confessed Michael. "'Get outta the way, it's my turn!' Pushing each other away to make room for ourselves."

"I saw something that really blew me away. I didn't know things like that existed," Michael recalled of his strangest experience in one of the clubs. "I had seen quite a few strippers, but that night this one girl with gorgeous eyelashes and long hair came out and did her routine. All of a sudden at the end, she took off her wig, pulled a pair of big oranges out of her bra, and revealed that she was a hard-faced guy under all that makeup. That blew me away. I was only a child and couldn't even conceive of anything like that."

Eventually, Joe Jackson became a part-time employee at the steel mill. Managing his sons became a full-time job. "When the show business thing became important to them," remembered Joe, "they started to make some money off it. I didn't want to deny them the opportunity to have this profession, and I didn't want them to be managed by a stranger who might let them run wild. So I quit my job at the steel mill and gave my time to the show business part of it."

"My father did always protect us and that's no small feat," remembered Michael. "He always tried to make sure people didn't cheat us. He looked after our interests in the best ways. He might have made a few mistakes along the way, but he always thought he was doing what was right for his family."

While Joe Jackson proved to be a competent manager, he was also a stern taskmaster. Michael feared his father. A disapproving look from Joe drew tremors from his sons.

After doing as many as 14 shows on a single weekend, the boys returned to Gary for school on Mondays. Following each trip, Joe gave his sons an extensive critique of their performance. While their father drove, the boys would study during the daylight hours, but when it became dark, the books were abandoned. Joe and his sons would drive through the night, singing either the traditional songs learned at home or current rhythm-and-blues hits. The monotony of the long rides was occasionally broken by a sock fight, but Joe would soon put an end to such antics. After finally falling to sleep, the brothers usually arrived in Gary at about four or five in the morning. It was often difficult for the boys to stay awake in school the next day.

Michael enjoyed the pillow fights and rough-housing with his brothers, but he was beginning to feel increasingly lonely and isolated, even from those who were closest to him. Many nights, he cried himself to sleep.

While life on the road was difficult, it also provided Michael with opportunities few 10-year-old

children experienced. "I would sit on stage at shows and watch James Brown and Jackie Wilson perform," he recalled. "I would watch and really feel it, particularly the crowd and the way they reacted. That's what I wanted to do. I felt it so much it seemed like I could just run up there and do what they did. I sat there every day and watched. . . . I'd stare at their feet, the way they held their arms, the way they gripped a microphone, trying to decipher what they were doing and why they were doing it. After studying James Brown from the wings, I knew every step, every grunt, every spin, and turn."

A shy 10-year-old off the stage, Michael was too nervous to introduce himself to the great black stars he routinely saw in the clubs. One night, Michael became fascinated with a hydraulically operated microphone that disappeared into the floor at the end

Along with thousands of other families across the country, the Jacksons were deeply saddened by the assassination of Dr. Martin Luther King, Jr.

of each performance. But he was too timid to ask the stagehands how it worked. When no one was around, he ventured into the theater's dreary basement to discover for himself where the microphone went.

Once that same microphone was placed in Michael's hands, however, an amazing transformation took place. "At that time Michael was the closest thing to James Brown you could find," remembered Don Cornelius of television's nationally syndicated "Soul Train." Freddie Perren, who would later produce the Jackson Five's first singles at Motown, recalled seeing the boys in 1968. "When I saw these little kids opening the show for us I really felt sorry for them and hoped the crowd would be kind to them," admitted Perren. "Michael was so little and innocent. You know how a crowd can be. Well, Michael just destroyed the audience. He was amazing, just an amazing performer. Hey, it was very rough trying to come on after that, let me tell you."

As in many African-American families, 1968 was also a year of tragedy for the Jacksons. The entire family was shocked and disturbed by the assassination of civil rights leader Martin Luther King, Jr., on April 4, in Memphis, Tennessee. "I remember so well the day he died," Michael later wrote. "Everyone was torn up. We didn't rehearse that night. I went to Kingdom Hall with Mom and some of the others. People were crying like they had lost a real member of their own family. I was too young to grasp the full tragedy of the situation, but when I look back on that day now, it makes me want to cry—for Dr. King, for his family, and for all of us."

But for Michael there were also plenty of good times and wishes and dreams for the future. "I remember going swimming as a child and making a wish before I jumped into the pool," he later told an interviewer. "Remember, I grew up knowing the industry, understanding goals, and being told what was and was not possible. I wanted to do something special. I'd stretch my arms out, as if I were sending my thoughts right up into space. I'd make my wish, then I'd dive into the water. I'd say to myself, 'This is my dream. This is my wish,' every time I'd dive into the water. I believe in wishes and in a person's ability to make a wish come true. I really do."

Michael's greatest wish was to create the biggest-selling record of all time. ✺

4

LAUNCHED BY MOTOWN

THE JACKSON FIVE hoped during 1968 that their debut record or one of their sold-out appearances would lead to a break, something to help them move to the next level of show business. One of their biggest goals was to perform at the Apollo Theater in the New York City district known as Harlem. Every Wednesday night, the Apollo held its legendary amateur-night competition. Vocalists Ella Fitzgerald, Sarah Vaughan, and Billie Holiday had all boosted their early careers by performing there. Winning at the Apollo could mean introductions to managers, booking agents, and record companies.

In the summer of 1968, the group finally received an invitation to appear at the Apollo. "We knew that if we could make it in New York, we could make it anywhere," wrote Michael. "That's what a win at the Apollo meant to us."

As the Jackson family received a guided tour of the stately old theater, Michael stared in awe at the pictures of all his favorite performers. Years later, he recalled peering beneath the stage curtains to watch these great acts. "They would all wear these beautiful

Located in Harlem in New York City, the Apollo Theater has been the mecca for African-American entertainers for more than 50 years. The Jackson Five's performance there in the summer of 1968 was the beginning of the band's rise to stardom.

patent-leather shoes," he remembered. "My whole dream seemed to center on having a pair of patent-leather shoes. I remember being so heartbroken because they didn't make them in little boys' sizes. Oh how I wanted some patent-leather shoes like the ones Jackie Wilson wore."

Filled with hope and anticipation before their performance, the Jackson Five were also frightened. If the Apollo audience did not like an act, people in the crowd would pummel the performer with cans and bottles. "There was this object just offstage which resembled a tree trunk which was supposed to bring good luck to first-time entertainers if you touch it before going on," Joe Jackson recalled. "Although the object was on stage behind the curtain, it was positioned so that most of the audience could see you touched it. I remember the kids touching it before they went on."

While arranging for his sons' performance at the Apollo, Joe Jackson had met a young lawyer, Richard Arons, a staffer at the musician's union. Jackson and Arons got along well, and Jackson asked the lawyer if he would be interested in helping to manage the boys. After watching the Jackson Five perform expertly at the Apollo, Arons could not wait to work with the group. During the next 10 years, Arons would use his experience in the music industry to handle negotiations for the group while Joe acted as spokesman for his sons.

Following their well-received performance at the Apollo, the Jacksons were delighted to receive an invitation to perform on "The David Frost Show," a nationally syndicated television program filmed in New York City. Michael told all the kids at school about the group's big break. Arriving home from school armed with lots of homework to take on the trip to New York, he was shocked to learn that his father had canceled the Frost show appearance. "I was ready to cry. We had been about to get our big break," Michael remembered. "I was reeling and I think everyone else was too. 'I cancelled it,' my father announced calmly, 'because Motown called.' A chill ran down my spine."

Michael Jackson knew very well that Motown was one of the few black-owned record companies in America. It was also among the most respected and most powerful recording labels. A former prize-fighter and record-store owner turned songwriter, Berry Gordy had employed an aggressive business approach to take himself to the very top of the music industry. Frustrated by his inability to achieve success as a songwriter for other companies, he had created his own record label in Detroit in 1959 and had taken on the established New York–based labels. Gordy's maneuver marked the first time that the major New York companies were successfully challenged by a small out-of-town house.

Gordy's success was no accident. A keen judge of talent, he rescued gifted kids from the streets and transformed them into legends. His discoveries over the years included Smokey Robinson, Diana Ross, the Temptations, and Stevie Wonder. He controlled every aspect of the company—from the most minute business details to the holding of songwriting royalties and the managing of all the acts. Gordy referred to his performers as his "students," and he put his young acts through a type of "Motown Charm School." He taught them etiquette, table manners, and how to conduct themselves in any situation. They learned how to sit properly and which silverware to use at the table.

Many conflicting stories exist surrounding Motown's discovery of the Jackson Five. Gladys Knight and the Pips, who were performing at the Apollo when the Jacksons first played there, later claimed that they had told Gordy about the group. Joe Jackson

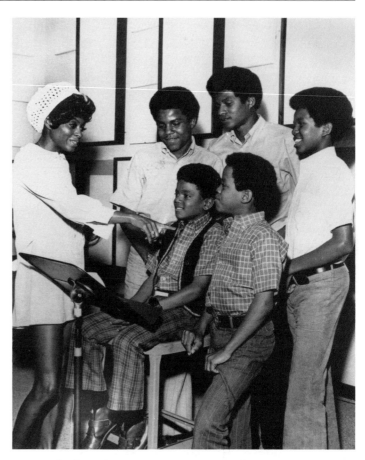

One of the country's most popular performers, Diana Ross was immediately impressed with the Jackson brothers, especially their young lead singer, Michael.

insisted that his first contact with Motown came through Bobby Taylor of the Vancouvers, although Joe admitted that "Gladys Knight had been talking to me about Motown for a year or so before I'd come in contact with Bobby Taylor."

Tom Noonan of *Billboard* magazine told yet another story. "Bobby Taylor had been talking about the Jackson Five," said Noonan, "but it wasn't until Diana Ross called Berry full of enthusiasm for these kids that Berry got interested. If anybody else had called I don't think it would have happened. Diana is the reason he got excited."

By 1968, Berry Gordy had been focusing much of his attention on moving the company's operations to

Los Angeles to include filmmaking in Motown's business expansion. Still, Motown desired a youthful discovery, for many of its groups had been launched in the early 1960s and now appealed to an older audience. Captivated by the Jackson Five, Gordy decided to mold them into a 1970s-style Motown group. Gordy invited the Jacksons to Detroit for an audition; Joe and his sons boarded their van once more, confident that they were going to surprise a few people.

Accustomed to an audience, the Jacksons were unnerved by the prospect of performing before only a small film crew at Hittsville, U.S.A., Motown's studio. When the boys completed their last number, "Who's Loving You," there was no applause, only silence. Although he had been coached to allow his father to do all the talking, Michael could not stand the suspense. Confused by the lack of reaction, he blurted out, "How was that?" One of the older backup players retorted, "Jackson Jive, huh?" Michael and his brothers did not know what to think. Driving home to Gary with their father, they wondered if it was the beginning—or the end—of their Motown connection.

Their answer came quickly. At Gordy's request, the band was flown to Detroit, where they auditioned at the poolside of the Motown owner's spacious mansion. Jackie Jackson later remembered that it was the biggest place they had ever seen. The backyard was like a golf course, and there was an indoor pool. Most of the Motown artists were there. Nervously, the Jackson Five launched into their songs. Following their performance, the Motown artists gave them a standing ovation. "Diana Ross came over at the end of the show and she kissed each one of us," Michael recalled. "She said she loved what she saw and wanted to be a part of what we do."

Although Motown made child singer Stevie Wonder a star in the early 1960s, the company had never recorded a kids' group. Yet Gordy was determined to create the type of group that would personify Motown's well-cultivated image. He gathered the boys together in a meeting and said, "I'm going to make you the biggest thing in the world and you're gonna be written about in history books. Your first record will be a number one, your second record will be a number one, and so will your third record. Three number one records in a row. You'll hit the charts just as Diana Ross and the Supremes did." Listening to this powerful man telling them they would make history, the boys felt as if they were living in a fairy tale. But Gordy's predictions would prove accurate.

Creating a successful group was going to take a lot of hard work and grooming. Gordy wished to begin the task immediately by moving the boys to Los Angeles, while Katherine and Joe Jackson re-turned to Gary. It took the family 18 months to sell its home and relocate permanently to California. During this period, Michael and his brothers were divided into groups, alternately staying with Berry Gordy and Diana Ross, who lived on the same Beverly Hills street.

"When we flew to California from Chicago, it was like being in another country, another world," Michael recalled. "To come from our part of Indiana, which is so urban and often bleak, and to land in Southern California was like having the world transformed into a wonderful dream. I was all over the place—Disneyland, Sunset Strip, the beach. We were awestruck by California; trees had oranges and leaves on them in the middle of winter. There were palm trees and beautiful sunsets, and the weather was so warm. . . . Those were heady days."

Following Motown's established practices, Gordy assigned a person to groom and shape the Jackson Five. Suzanne dePasse of Motown became the group's manager. She soon had the boys sporting huge round

Before signing the Jackson Five, Motown's Berry Gordy had only worked with one other child star, singer-composer Stevie Wonder. Wonder would remain a major figure in popular music for the next two decades, often performing with the Jackson Five.

hairdos known as Afros and brightly colored psyche-delic clothes. She taught them manners and grammar and prepped them for the coming media blitz through question-and-answer drills.

Shortly after the boys arrived in Los Angeles, Diana Ross hosted an exclusive private party at the Daisy Club to welcome the Jackson Five to their new home and to introduce them to people in the music business and the press. Recalling the group's early relationship with Motown's premier star, Michael later wrote, "She was so wonderful, mothering us and making us feel right at home. Most of the time I'd spend the day at Diana's and the night at Berry's. This was an important part of my life because Diana loved art and encouraged me to appreciate it too."

Ross took Michael to museums and introduced him to the works of Michelangelo and Degas. She bought the young singer pencils and paints and spent hours with him painting. "She was my mother, my lover, and my sister all combined in one amazing person," Michael said.

"In this young boy she saw all of her early ambition and desire," wrote biographer Nelson George. "And to Michael, Diana was the epitome of success. The hours they shared together then, and over the next decade, had a profound effect on Michael." With the Jackson Five's first album, *Diana Ross Presents the Jackson Five*, Motown placed its stamp of success on this new group from Gary.

Gordy sought the perfect sound for the Jackson Five's first hit single. He found it in "I Want You Back," written by Freddie Perren, who had seen the Jackson Five in Chicago a few years earlier and had worried at the time that audiences might be cruel to such a young child as Michael. Gordy and Perren were determined that the boys' debut would receive an enthusiastic response. The band practiced around the clock, working with professional dance instructors to polish their stylish choreography.

Regina Jones of *Soul* magazine later remembered the Jackson children as "some of the best mannered, well behaved I've ever met, in or out of show business. They had been well trained. Had great manners." Of Michael, Jones was even more complimentary. "We took them out for a photo shoot in a park in Los Angeles," she recalled, "and it wasn't long before they were out there playing basketball. Michael wouldn't play. He preferred to sit there and talk. He'd ask questions about everything. He could be in a crowd at their house with groups of people around and just sit there with his sketch pad drawing. You could see he was a thoughtful, sensitive child."

Michael spent most of his time either studying or working. Each day he spent three hours with a tutor, after which he would report to the recording studio, where he would work for hours until it was bedtime. There was a park across the street from the recording studio, and Michael could hear the children playing as he worked. But the young star had little time for friends and normal childhood activities. His only friends were his brothers.

During the band's first day in the studio, the Jackson Five's performance of "I Want You Back" went so well that a rough mix was quickly made and taken over to Gordy's apartment that same afternoon. Pleased with their work, the brothers felt they would be home in time for dinner. But Gordy was not satisfied with what he heard. It was one o'clock in the morning when he finally allowed the sleepy Jacksons to stop working and go home.

The group performed the number again and again, as Gordy attempted to determine what needed improvement. After listening to each brother sing alone, Gordy called 10-year-old Michael aside. "He told me exactly what he wanted and how he wanted me to help him get it," recalled Michael. "Berry was brilliant in that area. That's the way Motown did things in those days because Berry insisted on perfection and attention to detail. I'll never forget his persistence. This was his genius. He could identify the little elements that would make a song great rather than just good. It was like magic, as if Berry was sprinkling pixie dust over everything."

Released in November 1969, "I Want You Back" sold 2 million copies in six weeks and went to number one as Gordy had predicted. But the Motown owner's gift for fortune-telling did not end there. "ABC," the group's second single, hit the pop charts the next March and sold 2 million copies in three weeks. In

The Jackson Five were still young and inexperienced when they first achieved national recognition. The brothers are pictured here in their first photograph after signing with Motown Records in 1969.

June 1970, the band's third single, "The Love You Save," also went to number one. Berry Gordy's prophecies proved to be completely on target. By the fall of 1971, when the Jacksons turned out their fourth straight hit, "I'll Be There," the Jackson Five had created a new sound for a new decade. It was the first time in recording history that a group of children had made so many hit records.

When "I Want You Back" hit the charts, Motown continued to groom the Jackson Five for even greater success. "We were still rehearsing daily and working hard—some things didn't change—but we were grateful to be where we were," Michael said. "There were so many people pulling for us, and we were so determined ourselves that it seemed anything could happen."

Berry Gordy continued to be the steering force behind the success of the Jacksons. He went from studio to studio, checking on every aspect of the work, often adding elements that made the records better. Michael soon learned how to tell when Gordy was enjoying the performance in the studio. The Motown owner would roll his tongue in his cheek when he was pleased by something. If things were really going well, he would punch the air like a prizefighter.

While the Jackson Five were topping the pop charts, other children's groups began to climb aboard the Jackson bandwagon. Groups such as the Osmonds, the Partridge Family, and the DeFranco Family already existed, but their styles were based on barbershop harmony. Trying to sound more like the Jackson Five, these groups quickly adopted a more soulful quality to their music. When the Jacksons' relatives heard another group's song, "One Bad Apple," they mistook the singers for the Jackson Five. But the brothers did not mind being imitated. They were on top. Everyone else was copying their style. All the hours of practicing had finally begun to pay off. ❦

5

THE PRICE OF STARDOM

THE LATE 1960s were turbulent years for America. The war in Vietnam and the assassinations of Robert Kennedy and Martin Luther King, Jr., created an era marked by public protests and tensions between blacks and whites. With their clean-cut image and positive performances, the Jackson Five represented another side of America. The band's overwhelming popularity reminded many citizens that success could still be achieved by anyone in the country.

The Jackson Five first appeared on national television in the 1969 Miss Black America beauty pageant. But their celebrated debut on CBS's "Ed Sullivan Show" was the first time that most Americans saw the band perform. An appearance on Ed Sullivan's show indicated that an act had finally reached the top.

The group began its set with "I Want You Back," and the crowd screamed as Tito, Jermaine, Marlon, and Jackie created a backdrop for Michael's performance. Dressed in bell-bottom trousers and a colorful vest, the 12-year-old vocalist delighted the audience with his spirited dancing and charming falsetto voice. Seeing Michael in the hall after the show, Ed Sullivan told him, "Never forget that God gave you this talent." It was a comment Michael never forgot.

With their positive attitude and clean-cut appearance, the Jackson Five offered their fans an alternative to the rebellious image presented by many other popular bands during the period.

The Jackson Five were first introduced to a national television audience on the "Ed Sullivan Show" in 1969.

The boys were naturals for television. Following their performance on the Sullivan show, they appeared on Johnny Carson's "Tonight Show," Dick Clark's "American Bandstand," and Don Cornelius's "Soul Train." Recalling his association with Cornelius, Michael later said, "He had been a local disc jockey during our Chicago days, so we all knew one another from that time. We enjoyed watching his show and picked up ideas from those dancers who were from our part of the country." Appearing on ABC's "Hollywood Palace," the Jackson Five shared billing with their friends Diana Ross and the Supremes.

Not only were the Jackson Five a hit on television, they quickly became the darlings of the print media as well. *Look, Life, Newsweek,* the *Saturday*

Evening Post, the *New York Times Magazine,* and *Rolling Stone* featured the incredible story of the Jackson family's meteoric rise to fame. Careful to cultivate the desired image, Motown played an important role in controlling the press's coverage of the Jackson Five by promoting both the individual brothers and the group in just the right light. "Looking back, I wouldn't say Motown was putting us in any kind of straitjacket or turning us into robots, even though I wouldn't have done it that way myself; and if I had children, I wouldn't tell them what to say," wrote Michael. "The Motown people were doing something with us that hadn't been done before, and who was to say what was the right way to handle that sort of stuff?"

While Jackie was portrayed as the gifted athlete, Tito was described as the loner who loved cars. Marlon was said to have created many of the group's dance steps, and Jermaine was considered to be the group's ladies' man. Michael was promoted as a sweet little cherub. His interest in drawing and his "little brother" role within the group were also promoted. From an early age, however, Michael was characterized by some observers as an old soul in a young body.

Any attempts to meld Michael into the group were ultimately futile. Michael was just too gifted a performer. From the beginning, everyone knew that he would be the group's chief attraction. It was Michael, with his sharply honed dance steps and angelic voice, that the crowds came to see.

In the fall of 1971, the Jackson Five launched a series of national tours. Fans around the country reacted with a level of enthusiasm unseen since the Beatles' invasion in 1964. At one performance in Milwaukee, Wisconsin, the band drew 115,000 people. After the show, a mob blocked the group's exit from the arena and forced them to leave the waterfront arena in a police boat. A newspaper account of another incident reported that 10 minutes prior to curtain time at New York City's Madison Square Garden, "the barrier was smashed like so many pieces of kindling wood before the idol-crazed charge of pre-teen and teenage girls." With order restored, the Jacksons were able to complete their act, but an arena official said the group could not return "unless the governor promises to bring out the National Guard."

Over the years, the band received numerous awards from *Billboard*, the National Academy of Recording Arts and Sciences (which presents the Grammy Awards), the National Urban League, and the National Association for the Advancement of Colored People. The group's most treasured honor came when it returned to Gary on January 31, 1971. While a blizzard with 40-mile-per-hour winds raged, the brothers performed at the Westside High School Field, where their arrival was greeted by nearly 1,000 devoted fans, and Gary mayor Richard Hatcher presented them with the key to the city. Performing with a support crew of 25 and more than a ton of equipment, the Jackson Five then put on two more shows in front of 16,000 jubilant Gary fans. Upon visiting their old home at 825 Jackson Street, the Jacksons saw a large banner hanging from the roof that read "Welcome Home Jackson Five."

Back in California, everything changed for the boys. No longer able to attend public schools due to the intrusions of maniacal fans, the brothers enrolled in private schools with other child entertainers and the children of stars. "I only went to one public school in my life," Michael later explained. "I tried to go to another one in Los Angeles, but it didn't work, because we'd be in our class and a bunch of fans would break into the classroom, or we'd come out of school and there would be a bunch of kids waiting to take pictures and stuff like that. We stayed at that school for a week. One week! That was all we could take."

Whenever fans learned the location of the Jacksons' home, things got wild. "They'd jump the fence and sleep in the yard and try to get inside the house," recalled Michael.

Increasingly, the Jacksons existed in a private world, sheltered from the deluge of public attention. Rarely allowed to go anywhere alone, they were always accompanied by a Motown public relations person during interviews.

But if the public and Motown viewed the Jackson Five as celebrities, Joe Jackson continued to see them as a normal family unit. He moved to the Hollywood Hills area and resumed his role as head of the household and strict disciplinarian. Allowances were routinely held back a week for uncompleted homework or for goofing off at rehearsals. Phone calls were limited to five minutes. "If you can't say what you need to in that time," Joe insisted, "you'd better sit down and think about what you're calling about before you use the phone." Seeking to escape the Hollywood limelight, Joe moved his family to a $250,000 estate in the wealthy San Fernando Valley community of Encino.

In contrast to their spartan home in Gary, the Jacksons' new home was a manor featuring orange trees and surrounded by high fences. The property was guarded by a closed-circuit television system, with a surveillance camera mounted on a 15-foot pole. The estate also featured a full-size basketball court and a large pool. The Jacksons added a $100,000 recording studio behind the house, where the boys wrote and recorded music, and a $25,000 darkroom to encourage Marlon and Michael's growing interest in photography.

Several of the Jacksons attended the Walton School, an alternative education school with five classrooms and limited enrollment. The student body was primarily composed of wealthy children and show-business kids. When the group toured, it was accompanied by a tutor, Rose Fine. "It was Rose who instilled in me a love of books and literature that sustains me today," recalled Michael. "I read everything I could get my hands on."

While touring, the Jackson brothers always enjoyed shopping in new cities. But their increasing popularity often made even that small pleasure impossible. Attempting to enter a department store, the brothers were mobbed by fans. Describing such a scene, Michael later remembered, "Counters would get knocked over, glass would break, the cash registers would be toppled. If you have not witnessed such a scene, you cannot imagine what it is like." The boys hired fake limos and impersonators to draw the crowds away so that they could slip unnoticed out of concert halls.

Suzanne dePasse, the Jackson Five's road manager, befriended a Harlem high school student, Steve Manning, and assigned him the task of answering the fan mail. Manning soon found that his room was stacked with mail. Fans sent not only letters but toys, rings, and candy. "The Jackson Five then were a very timely group for black Americans. It was the time of Afro and black pride," Manning recalled. "Never before had black teenagers had someone to idolize like that." Typically, many letters from female fans offered marriage proposals, while many of the letters from young men simply wanted to know how the Jackson Five maintained their Afro hairdos.

Manning later described the first time he met the Jacksons, in Philadelphia in 1971. "I waited in the hotel lobby for them to bring me upstairs," he recalled, "and there were hundreds of people, hundreds of girls, lingering there looking for some way up to the group's room. My initial reaction was

In 1972, 14-year-old Michael sang the title song for the popular motion picture Ben. *It was the first time that the singer had released a recording without the help of his brothers.*

surprise that Michael was really just a little boy." Although Michael was a celebrity, he remained childlike when out of the limelight. Offstage, he ran around, painted with watercolors, and played with animals. When he was performing, a chameleonlike change took place. Once the spotlight cast its glow upon him, the 14-year-old instantly became an adult.

During the summer of 1971, the Jacksons starred in their first network television special, "Goin' Back to Indiana." The show featured entertainers Bill Cosby, Diana Ross, Tommy Smothers, and Bobby Darin. It also featured film clips of the band's hit concert in Gary. A Saturday-morning Jackson Five cartoon series also aired that summer.

In 1972, the release of Michael's single "Ben," the title song to an unusual horror movie of the same name, dwarfed any earlier fame that the young singer had achieved. The movie starred Lee Harcourt Mont-

Motown Records founder Berry Gordy was one of the most powerful figures in the recording industry during the 1960s and 1970s. He worked carefully with the Jackson Five, transforming Michael into a major star.

gomery in the role of a young man who raised pet rats. The song illustrated the friendship that developed between the main character of the movie and an extremely intelligent rat. Michael sang the song with such sensitivity and conviction that it seemed as if the words were his own. The song quickly became Michael's signature piece. He later told an interviewer with *Crawdaddy* magazine, "I love rats, you know, like in *Ben*. I really do feel like I'm talking to a friend when I play with them. I used to raise them at home."

By 1972, the Jacksons' fame had spread throughout the world. Embarking on an international tour, the group appeared at a Silver Jubilee celebration in

Great Britain, giving a command performance for Queen Elizabeth II at King's Hall in Glasgow, Scotland. They were one of the youngest pop groups ever to perform for the royal family. Continuing their European tour, the Jackson Five performed in sold-out concert halls in Italy, Germany, and France. The tour also provided Michael with his first visits to historic art galleries and broadened his interest in art.

Large crowds greeted the Jacksons in Asia as well. In Japan, they performed in Tokyo, Osaka, and Hiroshima. The aborigines of Australia believed that the band members were brothers from across the sea and hosted the Jacksons at an honorary cookout. Michael later recalled how the brothers were greeted by dancers when they first landed in Africa. "There was a long line of Africans dancing in their native costumes, with drums and shakers," he said. "They were really into it. What a perfect way to welcome us to Africa."

But the group's intense work schedule had begun to have an effect on Michael. On one occasion, the whole family was packed and ready to leave for a South American tour, but Michael was missing. After hours of searching, the others finally found him hiding and crying; he wanted to go outside to play, not get on another airplane.

As Michael became a seasoned performer, he gained more confidence in his creative intuition. In the early days at Motown, a group called the Corporation guided the Jackson Five and wrote and produced their first singles. Composed of Freddy Perren, Bobby Taylor, Deke Richards, Hal Davis, and Fonce Mizell, the Corporation molded the Jackson sound. Although Michael often disagreed with their decisions concerning the music, he had remained silent and obedient.

In 1972, everything changed. Working on the song "Lookin' Through the Windows," Michael

Even as a very young man, Michael possessed a confidence in himself as an artist that belied his seeming youthful naïveté.

challenged the Corporation's production of the number. "They wanted me to sing a certain way and I knew they were wrong," Michael explained. "No matter what age you are, if you have it and you know it, then people should listen to you. I was furious with our producers and very upset."

Michael immediately called Berry Gordy and complained that the Corporation's sound was becoming too mechanical. Gordy instructed the producers to allow Michael to do what he wanted to do. Following that incident, Michael began to add vocal twists, infusing his words with an individual style that proved to be very popular.

When Michael Jackson was 14, his appearance began to change. For one thing, he was growing noticeably taller. People often failed to recognize him and sometimes mistook him for someone else. Expecting a cute, charming child, they discovered instead a gangly adolescent who was nearly 5 feet 10 inches tall. Then Michael developed a terrible case of acne. Depressed about his appearance, he was extremely embarrassed for anyone to see him. He did not even want to look at himself. He washed his face in the dark, avoiding mirrors. "The effect on me was so bad that it messed up my whole personality," Michael said of this painful period in his life. "I couldn't look at people when I talked to them. I would look down or away."

Yet when Michael was on the stage, he did not think of anything else but performing. He could forget about his appearance because he was proud of his music. Eventually, he was able to control the acne through a change in his diet.

Each personal and professional obstacle that Michael encountered resulted in a growing trust in his own judgment. Michael Jackson was gradually emerging as the great talent he always knew he could be. ◆◖◗◆

6

DANCING TO HIS OWN TUNE

❧

THE RELATIONSHIP BETWEEN the Jackson Five and Motown Records began to come apart in 1973. Despite a successful hit, "Get It Together," the band members felt frustrated by Motown's continued tight control of their lives. "We were growing up and we were expanding creatively," explained Michael Jackson. "We had so many ideas we wanted to try out, but they were convinced that we should not fool with a successful formula."

In 1974, the Jacksons enjoyed the most sophisticated hit of their career, "Dancing Machine." Michael loved the groove and the feel of the song, and he was determined to find just the right dance move to accompany it. Performing "Dancing Machine" on "Soul Train," he introduced a street-style step called the Robot. Immediately, "Dancing Machine" soared to the top of the charts. Suddenly, it seemed that every teenager in the country was doing the Robot.

That same year, Motown told the Jackson Five that they would not be allowed to write their own songs. "They not only refused to grant our requests, they told us it was taboo to even mention that we wanted to do our own music," Michael wrote. Confronting Berry Gordy with his frustrations, Michael protested the band's lack of creative freedom. Unable

By the early 1970s, creative differences had begun to strain the relationship between the Jackson Five and Motown Records. Following the release of their 1974 hit, "Dancing Machine," the band left Motown to sign with Epic Records.

On December 15, 1973, Jermaine Jackson married Berry Gordy's daughter Hazel Joy Gordy. When the Jackson Five left Motown Records the following year, Jermaine supported his new father-in-law and stayed with the label.

to come to an agreement, the Jackson Five decided to move to Epic Records. The brothers were saddened, however, when Jermaine, who had married Gordy's daughter, announced that he would stay with Motown. It was difficult for the group to continue without Jermaine, so Randy officially joined the group, replacing Michael as the baby of the band. These changes also ushered in the group's new name, the Jacksons. Motown refused to relinquish its rights to the name the Jackson Five.

Ironically, it was Michael Jackson's association with Motown that provided the next new venture of his career: acting in a film. In 1977, Motown secured the rights to the Broadway musical *The Wiz* for Diana Ross. Jackson jumped at the chance to act alongside Ross and auditioned for the part of the Scarecrow. When he heard that the part was his, he felt both exhilarated and scared. He realized that the movie would require his full attention and the Jacksons would have to continue without him for several months.

Michael quickly adjusted to life in New York City, where the film was shot. "Making *The Wiz* was an education for me on so many levels," he said. "As a recording artist I already felt like an old pro, but the film world was completely new to me." Now 19, Michael Jackson was making decisions about the creative paths his career would take, and his experiences on the set of *The Wiz* helped him to formulate his plans.

Jackson also learned that he loved the effects of the heavy makeup that he had to wear for the role. While most other actors detested the four hours a day that it took to apply and remove the extensive makeup, he enjoyed it. Still concerned about his complexion, he liked the fact that the makeup completely covered his blemishes and gave him the delightful feeling of really becoming transformed. When children came up to him on the set, he was not Michael Jackson; he was the Scarecrow.

Above all, Jackson loved the idea of portraying a character other than himself. His thorough disguise allowed him to experience what it was like to become a completely different person. His wig was made of steel wool pads, and a peanut butter cup covered his nose. "I loved everything about the costume, from the coil legs to the tomato nose to the fright wig," Jackson said.

The intricate choreography provided Michael Jackson with yet another challenge. Unlike many of the other actors, he possessed the uncanny ability to see a move once and then be able to perform it. Rehearsing with Diana Ross and the actors playing the Tin Man and the Lion, Jackson felt perplexed when the other actors became irritated with him. Finally, Ross took him aside and explained that it was frustrating to the rest of the cast to be so easily upstaged. "We laughed about it," recalled Jackson, "but I tried to make the ease with which I learned my steps less obvious."

Unlike the movie on which it was based, *The Wizard of Oz*, *The Wiz* did not feature a fairy-tale

In 1976, Michael and the other Jacksons starred in four summer specials for CBS television.

kingdom. It was based more on reality, set in places with which children could identify, such as schoolyards, subway stations, and city neighborhoods. Jackson's favorite scene was the one in which Ross says, "What am I afraid of? Don't know what I'm made of . . ." "I have felt that way many times," he later confessed, "even during the good moments of my life."

When Jackson turned 21 in 1979, he took complete charge of his own business affairs and career decisions. Until that time, Joe Jackson had served as Michael's personal manager; but when Joe Jackson's contract expired that year, it was not renewed. In the past, Joe had made some statements that had embarrassed Michael, including one that Michael and many other people considered racist. "I happen to be color blind," Michael said to reporters in a public rebuttal of his father's words. "I don't hire color; I hire competence. The individual can be of my organization, but I have the final word on every decision. Racism is not my motto. One day I strongly expect every color to live as one family."

Discussing the decision to dismiss his father as manager, Michael stated bluntly, "I just did not like the way certain things were being handled. Mixing family and business can be a delicate situation. . . . All I wanted was control over my own life. And I took it."

Michael was also outgrowing the group. He was changing as an individual and as an artist. But the changes within him were not the only ones brewing in the family. In 1982, Joe and Katherine Jackson initiated divorce proceedings.

While on the set of The Wiz, Michael Jackson had met the music producer Quincy Jones. On one occasion, Jackson asked Jones if he could recommend a good producer for his next album. "Why don't you let me do it?" Jones replied. Jones had been impressed with Jackson's business knowledge. Unlike many recording artists who relied heavily on agents to handle their finances, Jackson knew exactly how much money he earned from the sale of each record in the United States and in each foreign country. He had not lumped his earnings in with the family's but had his own accountants and lawyers to manage his money from the Jacksons' records and tours.

The album *Off the Wall* was released in August 1979. It was the first of many projects on which Jackson and Jones collaborated during the next few years. While guiding the project with superb professional expertise, Jones allowed the arrangers and musicians broad creative freedoms. The album contained a pleasing balance of songs, including pieces written by Rod Temperton, Paul and Linda McCartney, and Michael Jackson. The recording combined moving ballads, such as "Girlfriend," "I Can't Help It," and the emotionally charged "She's Out of My Life," with up-tempo dance music such as "Don't Stop 'Til You Get Enough," "Working Day and Night," "Get on the Floor," and "Rock with You." The music appealed to a wide range of listeners.

Jackson had a wonderful time working with Jones on *Off the Wall*. Outside of the studio, however, the young singer was going through one of the most difficult periods of his life. "I had very few close friends at the time and felt very isolated," he later revealed. Lonely, he would walk the streets, hoping to meet someone who would not recognize him as a celebrity—someone who would like him just for being himself. Jackson, who had dated occasionally, developed a close relationship with actress Tatum O'Neal. But his work demanded most of his time and attention, and he continued to feel lonely and alienated.

Jackson was extremely proud of *Off the Wall*, and he was stung when the album received only one

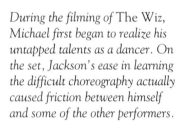

During the filming of The Wiz, *Michael first began to realize his untapped talents as a dancer. On the set, Jackson's ease in learning the difficult choreography actually caused friction between himself and some of the other performers.*

Grammy nomination—for best rhythm-and-blues vocal performance. He vowed that the voters would not be able to ignore his next album. Even so, the fans loved the album, which eventually sold nearly 6 million copies in the United States.

Following the completion of *Off the Wall*, Jackson dove into the making of the *Triumph* album with his brothers prior to the Jacksons' 1981 nationwide tour. Working with magician Doug Henning, the band developed a stage show featuring elaborate special effects. Following the performance of "Don't Stop 'Til You Get Enough," for instance, Michael completely disappeared in a huge puff of smoke.

When the Jacksons completed their tour, Michael vowed that it would be his last. "I love being on stage, but I don't like the other things that go with touring," he told Robert Hilburn of the *Los Angeles Times*. Although he never made an official announcement, *The Jacksons Live*, the two-record live album recorded during the 1981 tour, was the last album he did with his brothers until 1984.

From the beginning, Jackson's association with Quincy Jones was magical. When Jackson decided to record his next album, there was no question who the producer would be. In Michael's mind, Jones was not only the best man for the job; he also knew the best musicians, engineers, and songwriters in the business. "He knew Los Angeles better than Mayor Bradley," Jackson explained, "and that's how he kept up on what was going on. He knew track records, who was booked, who would be too lax, and who would put the 'pedal to the metal.'. . . He had a world of talent to choose from among his contacts, and he was a good listener, as well as a brilliant man."

Jackson's dream continued to be to make the biggest-selling album of all time. In 1981, he set out to realize that dream. Collaborating with Jones, he embarked on the most exciting project of his career. Speaking about Jackson's dedication, Quincy observed, "When he commits to an idea, he goes all the way with it. . . . It's a long way from idea to execution. Everybody wants to go to heaven and nobody wants to die." Jackson finally reached for heaven when he made *Thriller*.

"Making the *Thriller* album was very hard work, but it is true that you only get out of something what you put into it." Jackson recalled. "I am a perfectionist; I'll work until I drop. . . . When I take on a project I really put my soul into it. I would die for it." Even before he began work on the project, he had already written one song, "Wanna Be Startin' Somethin'." Benefiting from the experiences of his *Off the Wall* album, he once again sought the help of Paul

As Jackson became more popular, he discovered that even his private life was the subject of headlines. Here, he dances with an unidentified partner at New York City's Studio 54 in 1977.

McCartney. The result of their joint efforts was the single "Say Say Say."

While Jackson worked with McCartney, Jones listened to the songs of other writers. Jones was aware of Michael's habit of writing songs and then being too shy to show them to anyone. As the *Thriller* project unfolded, Jones cornered Jackson and demanded that the singer play him his latest composition. "Come on. Where is it? I know you got it," Jones insisted. The song was "Beat It." Jackson later remembered the first time that he played the song for Jones.

"He went crazy," said Michael. "I felt on top of the world." Written with school kids in mind, "Beat It" expressed Jackson's belief in nonviolence. Turned off by much of the music he had been hearing on the Top 40 charts, he had wanted to write the kind of song that he himself would go out and buy. Its message to street kids was simple: if someone is killed through fighting, everyone loses. Eddie Van Halen provided an incredible guitar solo performance that became the signature for the piece.

The third song that Jackson wrote for *Thriller*, "Billie Jean," was about a young man denying that he was the father of a child. "A musician knows his material. It has to feel right," he later wrote. "Everything has to feel in place. It fulfills you and makes you feel good. You know it when you hear it. That's how I felt about 'Billie Jean.' I knew it was going to be big while I was writing it."

"A lot of people have asked me about that song, and the answer is very simple," explained Jackson. "It's just a case of a girl who says that I'm the father of her child and I'm pleading my innocence because 'the kid is not my son.' There was never a real Billie Jean." The song represented a composite of the overly aggressive female fans who had harassed him and his brothers for years.

In making *Thriller*, Jackson produced three videos to support the recording. *Thriller*, the video, was a minimovie that broke new ground for videos with a story that had a beginning, a middle, and an end. The *Thriller* video cost $1.2 million—more than had ever been spent on making a video—and helped to sell a million albums a week in the month following its airing. Along with *Thriller*, promotional videos for "Billie Jean" and "Beat It" rejuvenated the entire recording industry. "Michael took the video from promotional gimmick into the realm of art form," noted biographer Caroline Latham.

Released in December 1982, the album *Thriller* immediately won critical acclaim and entered *Billboard* magazine's charts as the number 11 album in the country. Almost a year later, in the fall of 1983, the recording was still in the Top 10. The *New York Times* said that the album was "superbly crafted . . . with a pervasive confidence infusing the album as a whole. *Thriller* suggests that Mr. Jackson's evolution as an artist is far from finished. He is, after all, only 24 years old."

Jackson rode a crest of success in 1983. On Monday, May 16, the two-hour prime-time special "Motown 25: Yesterday, Today, and Forever" was broadcast. "After that," said Michael, "many things changed."

Almost 50 million people saw Jackson perform that night, and across the country people were suddenly talking about the Michael Jackson phenomenon. A number of articles were written about the singer's clothing, including his single glove, his white socks, and the way his pants legs ended high above his ankles. "I admit I love starting trends," Jackson later said, "but I never thought wearing white socks was going to catch on. . . . You can not think about these things: you have to feel your way into them. . . . My attitude toward fashion says if it is forbidden, I am going to do it." Many viewers in the Motown special's television audience also went out and bought the album. By 1988, *Thriller* had sold 8 million copies.

During the same year, the video *The Making of Thriller* was produced. In its cassette form, the video sold a million copies; it still holds the record as the best-selling music video of all time.

Another project Jackson undertook in 1983 was the renovation of his Encino home. A lover of art since Diana Ross had first introduced him to the subject, he added an art gallery to his home that featured works by his friend Andy Warhol. Loving the fantasy world of Disneyland, Jackson set aside a large room to recreate one of his favorite amusement park rides: the Pirates of the Caribbean ride in the Magic Kingdom. Disney engineers installed buccaneers, guns, cannons, and tropical scenery. Jackson's huge backyard featured his own private zoo with two fawns, a llama named Louis, macaws, cockatoos, and Michael's eight-foot boa constrictor, Muscles. By creating his own favorite places, Jackson could visit the zoo and Disneyland in the privacy of his own home.

When asked if he was happy, Jackson answered, "I do not think I am ever totally happy. . . . What really makes me happy, what I love is performing and creating. I really do not care about all the material trappings. I love to put my soul into something and have people accept it and like it. That's a wonderful feeling."

7

RECORD-BREAKING
RECORDS

❧

MICHAEL JACKSON'S CREATIVE endeavors may have been ignored prior to *Thriller*, but the awards bestowed upon him in 1984 erased any doubts about how highly he was regarded. He attended the American Music Awards in mid-January at the Houston Astrodome with Brooke Shields, a popular young actress and model. Michael and Brooke were the most photographed couple of the 200,000 people in attendance. Sixty million people watched on television as he walked away with eight awards, including a special Award of Merit. He became the youngest performer ever to win the award.

Brooke Shields also accompanied Michael to the Grammy Awards, where they were seated in the front row, with Jackson wearing a sequined military uniform with his trademark spangled glove. The night truly belonged to him. Making eight trips to the podium, he accepted more awards than anyone in the history of the Grammy Awards. Mickey Rooney, one of the presenters, quipped, "It is a pleasure doing the Michael Jackson show."

Although Michael's parents sat together in the audience that evening, they were no longer married. Michael was saddened by his parents' divorce. He had always been close to his mother, and he had recently

With the success of Thriller, *Jackson became the most popular entertainer in the world.*

had her home remodeled as a Swiss chalet. For her birthday in 1984, he presented her with a red Rolls-Royce all tied up with a white ribbon. The influence of Joe Jackson on Michael's career was obvious to everyone, but Katherine Jackson had stayed behind the scenes. According to biographer Nelson George, "It was Katherine Jackson who exercised the strongest influence on Michael's personal development."

Michael's public relations assistant Steve Manning agreed. "The softness and humbleness you find in Michael comes directly from her," Manning said. Michael and his mother continued to attend the yearly Jehovah's Witnesses' assembly at Dodger Stadium. (Michael and his sister Maureen were the only two Jackson children to be baptized as Jehovah's Witnesses.)

Michael and his father disagreed on some matters, but they both agreed about the importance of the family. Despite the fact that Michael did not like to travel, he agreed to embark on a 1984 tour with his brothers. The Jacksons selected boxing impresario Don King to promote the tour. Michael made sure he had control over various aspects of the tour, such as the orchestra, the music, the dancing, and the songs. Although Pepsi would sponsor the tour, Jackson made it clear that he would not drink the product as part of the promotional advertising. He had always felt that entertainers were exploited by that type of advertising.

As part of the Pepsi promotions, Michael and his brothers filmed Pepsi commercials, which were choreographed by Michael Peters, who had done the choreography for the *Thriller* video. The first commercial depicted the Jacksons walking down the street and bumping into a little boy imitating Michael Jackson.

The second commercial was more elaborate; shot in the Shrine Auditorium in Los Angeles, it showed

During the early 1980s, Jackson rarely had time for dating. One of his favorite companions when he did appear in public, however, was actress-model Brooke Shields.

the Jacksons in concert. Four hundred children were given free tickets to watch the performance. The scene called for the Jackson brothers to be performing on stage, where Michael would join them from a cloud of colored smoke created with the use of flash powder. There were technical problems, however. The smoke was too thin. More flash powder was added, and Merlin comets were used to ignite the powder. As Michael started down the stairs, there was an unexpected flash. The hair on the back of his head suddenly caught on fire.

As Michael began to scream, his bodyguard, Miko Brando, threw him to the floor and extinguished the flames with a jacket. Someone else immediately called an ambulance. Brando's quick response to the accident spared Michael from serious injuries. In the ambulance, Jackson insisted upon wearing his one white glove. Rushed to the emergency room of Cedars-Sinai Medical Center, he was examined by Dr. Steven Hoffman, who arranged for Michael to be transferred to a burn center. After the story was reported by newspapers, radio, and television stations, thousands of teenagers telephoned and sent letters. From around the world, people expressed their concern. One radio station received over 300 letters daily. Four million copies of *Thriller* were sold in the days following the accident.

Although Jackson wound up with a three-inch circle of burned flesh on the back of his head, he was released from the burn center just 18 hours after the accident. In mid-April, he underwent laser surgery to reconstruct the burned spot. Edited to remove the accident scene, the commercial was first shown during the 1984 Grammy Awards. As a result of the accident, Pepsi paid Jackson $1,500,000, which he immediately donated to the Michael Jackson Burn Center.

In addition to the Pepsi commercials, the Jacksons were working on a new album to be released before the start of their tour. Completed in May 1984, the album was called *Victory*, and the tour became the Victory tour. "I felt very powerful in those days," recalled Michael. "I felt on top of the world. I felt determined. That tour was like: 'We are a mountain. We have come to share our music with you. We have something we want to tell you.'" Each performance began with the Jacksons rising out of the stage and walking down a flight of stairs. Bright and imaginative, the opening number captured the spirit of the show, and the fans went wild.

Once again, the Jackson brothers were reunited. Jermaine had rejoined the group, and the Jacksons were riding a tide of public adulation. Although the response was overwhelmingly positive, Michael, always a perfectionist, was not entirely satisfied with the show. Despite his misgivings, he poured his heart and soul into each performance. Describing the thrill of performing, he later said, "Once I get to the side of the stage, something happens. The rhythm starts and the lights hit me and the problems disappear. It is like God saying, 'Yes, you can. Yes, you can. Just wait. Wait till you hear this.' And the beat gets in my backbone and it vibrates and it just takes me." Often, when the music "took Michael," he would change the direction of a performance, altering the order of songs or singing a song in a different way than he had practiced it. The musicians immediately had to adjust to his new routine. "The song takes you in another direction," he explained.

Following the tour, Jackson jumped at an opportunity to be involved with an exciting new project. Disney Studios asked Michael to design a new ride for their parks, and he responded with enthusiasm and met the Disney producers. "I told them that Walt Disney was a hero of mine," he said of his meeting, "and that I was interested in Disney's history and philosophy." Michael eventually agreed to appear in a film with Disney Studios to be shown in their parks. He told the producers that he would like to work with directors George Lucas and Steven Spielberg. When Spielberg was unable to participate, another well-known director, Francis Ford Coppola, was invited to be a part of the creative team.

Jackson met with Lucas at his Skywalker Ranch, where the two devised the idea for a short film that would utilize the most recent advances in three-dimensional technology. Their concept called for the audience to feel as though they were riding in a spaceship. Lucas called the film *Captain Eo*. (*Eo* is

During the 1980s, Jackson and composer-producer Quincy Jones forged one of the most celebrated creative partnerships in the history of American recording.

the Greek word for dawn.) "*Captain Eo* is about transformation and the way music can help to change the world," Jackson explained.

The film was the story of a young man who is given the mission of taking light and beauty to the inhabitants of an unhappy planet ruled by a wicked queen. Its theme conveyed the victory of good over evil. While the first half of the 17-minute film was reminiscent of a *Star Wars* space battle, the second portion featured Jackson emerging from a rickety spaceship to do battle with the evil queen. The filmmakers used special effects to transform a robot into a rock band. A leg became a guitar, and the torso became a drum, accompanying Jackson in an electrically charged performance of "We Are Here to Change the World."

Jackson's involvement with *Captain Eo* inspired him to learn more about films. Always a movie buff, he was also interested in photography. He enjoyed every aspect of filmmaking. When a director required a scene to be shot many times to capture the perfect light, Jackson was fascinated by the process. Similarly, he wanted to learn all he could about the changes being made in the script during the shooting. "It's all part of what I consider my ongoing education in films," observed Jackson. "Working on *Captain Eo* reinforced all the positive feelings I have had working on film and made me realize more than ever that movies are where my future path probably lies."

In early 1985, Jackson embarked on yet another exciting venture. Deeply disturbed by seeing the news footage of starving people in Ethiopia and the Sudan, he decided to help. With fellow entertainer Lionel Richie, he wrote the anthem "We Are the World."

One day, Michael asked his sister Janet to listen with him to the interesting acoustics in his bathroom. Singing only a single note with no lyrics, Michael asked Janet what feeling the note evoked. "What do you see," he asked, "when you hear this sound?" She replied, "Dying children in Africa." "You are right," Michael agreed. "That is what I was dictating from my soul." Next, he took Janet to a darkroom and sang "We Are the World" to her. "That's where 'We Are the World' came from," he later explained.

Once again, Jackson elicited the help of his friend Quincy Jones. The two men set up an all-night taping session to begin immediately after the American Music Awards ceremony. With the cast of star performers already assembled in Los Angeles for the awards ceremony, it was a wonderful opportunity for an all-star session. Dressed in casual clothes and standing on risers, America's top singers united their voices under Jones's direction. The huge choir of stars swayed in rhythm with the music as they sang the moving lyrics. When the video was released to the public, it was a smashing success, raising millions of dollars for the relief effort in Africa.

Following completion of "We Are the World" in 1985, Jackson went into seclusion for two and a half years while he worked on his follow-up project to *Thriller*. Working together, Quincy Jones and Michael decided that their next project would be as close to perfection as was humanly possible. The album, to be titled *Bad*, was not to be rushed in any sense. "A perfectionist has to take his time," Jackson explained. "He shapes and he molds and he sculpts that thing until it is perfect."

Throughout the recording of *Bad*, Jackson and Jones continued to enjoy a unique creative relationship. "What I do is, I write the songs and do the music and then Quincy brings out the best in me," Jackson said at the time. "That is the only way I can explain it." Jackson and Jones trusted one another completely. When Jones suggested a change, Jackson took the advice. Conversely, Jones granted Jackson broad creative liberties. The two men sometimes disagreed about drum sounds, but their differences were always in the spirit of producing the best possible work. The only tensions that arose stemmed from their relentless drive for perfection.

Continuing to develop as a composer, Jackson wrote all but two of the songs on *Bad*. The title song is about a street kid from a rough inner-city neighborhood who is sent to a private school. When he returns to his old neighborhood, the other kids begin to give him trouble. Expressing the view that strength and goodness are "bad," he sings, "I'm bad, you're bad, who's bad, who's the best?" In the spellbinding musical video made to accompany "Bad,"

Jackson used actual street gang members for the electrifying dance routines.

Another of Jackson's favorite songs from the recording was "Man in the Mirror," written by Siedah Garret and George Ballard. "If John Lennon was alive," observed Jackson, "he could really relate to that song because it says that if you want to make the world a better place, you have to work on yourself and change first. It's the same thing [John F.] Kennedy was talking about when he said, 'Ask not what your country can do for you; ask what you can do for your country.' That's the truth. That's what Martin Luther King meant and [Mohandas] Gandhi too. That's what I believe."

Despite his immense success, wealth, and fame at age 30, Jackson remained a lonely individual. "The things I share with millions of people are not the sort of things you share with one," he admitted sadly in 1988. "Many girls want to know what makes me tick—why I live or do the things I do—trying to get inside my head. They want to rescue me from my loneliness, but they do it in such a way that they give me the impression they want to share my loneliness, which I would not wish on anybody, because I believe I am one of the loneliest people in the world." •◡•

In spite of all the publicity about his private life, the most compelling image of Jackson is that of a man alone on the stage.

8

KING OF POP

DURING AN AWARDS show in 1989, Michael Jackson's friend Elizabeth Taylor introduced him as "the king of pop, rock, and soul." Fans immediately adopted the new nickname, displaying "King of Pop" banners at Jackson's concerts, and the phrase began to show up on T-shirts around the country. Wherever Jackson toured, fans gathered outside his hotel and chanted, "King of pop . . . king of MTV." Everyone agreed that Jackson was the dominant figure in popular music during the 1980s. The singer's albums *Thriller* and *Bad* were the two best-selling albums of the decade, and his concerts sold more tickets than those of any other performer.

When Jackson's *Black or White* video aired in 1991, it caused the biggest controversy of anything he had ever done. In the 11-minute video, one of the gestures he made was to grab his crotch repeatedly; the project also contained more scenes of violence than any video he had made in the past. Critics condemned the video's lack of good taste, and Jackson immediately cut four minutes from it to appease his fans.

Meanwhile, Quincy Jones was no longer around to give the singer advice. In fact, all of the personnel with whom Jackson had worked with earlier had been replaced. The star was now in complete control of all his creative and business decisions.

By the end of 1991, Jackson and his sister Janet were competing to outdo each other's remarkable

Jackson's love for animals has long been a favorite topic of his fans. Here, the singer poses with the black panther used in his controversial video Black or White.

89

This is how a Michael Jackson concert looks from the singer's perspective. More than 30,000 fans filled Rome's Flaminio soccer stadium at the start of Jackson's 1988 world tour.

achievements. A few days after Janet signed the richest recording deal in history, with Virgin Records, Michael topped her with his own $1 billion deal with the Sony Corporation. Later in the year, the two became the first brother-sister pair to turn out back-to-back number one pop hits.

Michael remained a perfectionist. He worked for four years on the album *Dangerous* and spent five times more money on the project than any recording artist had ever spent in the past. He refused to release a song unless it sounded exactly the way he wanted it to sound. During the recording sessions, he often became frustrated to the point of tears. As his musical ideas became increasingly complex, it became harder and harder to transfer the sounds in his head onto the tapes in the studio.

There was more to Jackson's life than music, however. In 1992, the singer established the Heal the World Foundation to raise and distribute funds to charities that aid children. That summer, he made a world tour, visiting 15 countries to raise money for the foundation.

Billed as the Dangerous tour, Jackson and his entourage visited cities not normally seen by pop stars. Opening in Munich, Germany, on June 27, he played before a crowd of 70,000 German fans. He ended the show in spectacular fashion, strapping on a jet-propelled backpack that shot him through the air and out of the stadium. The two-hour show, featuring hits from his four solo albums, broke box-office records throughout Europe and Africa. In addition, the concert in Bucharest, Rumania, on October 10, was filmed for HBO and earned Michael an unprecedented $20 million.

Around the world, Jackson's albums were still selling at a record pace. With more than 42 million copies sold worldwide, *Thriller* had easily become the biggest seller of all time. *Dangerous*—released in November 1991 on the performer's own label, Epic Records—sold more than 14 million copies in less than a year. It was the fastest-selling album in his career.

For all his achievements, Michael Jackson could not escape the challenge of topping himself. If *Thriller* sold 42 million copies, he wondered, could *Dangerous* sell 100 million? Truly a world star, he sold more than twice as many albums in the rest of the world as in North America.

But Jackson paid a price for his stardom. In order to achieve any level of privacy, he had to abandon hope of having a normal life. Even if he stayed home and never went out, the outside world tried to come to him. Photographers climbed trees outside his property, hoping to take a snapshot of him that could be sold to a magazine. Everywhere he went, everything he did was noted by somebody and printed—the things he bought, the restaurants where he ate, the movies he attended— nothing was too trivial for print. Jackson could no longer go to a mall, Disneyland, a movie theater, the zoo, or an art gallery without causing a disturbance.

Jackson, however, had the money to provide all those things for himself. If he could no longer visit his favorite places, he could bring the places to him. In the Santa Ynez Valley, an hour north of Santa

Unable to enjoy his favorite pastimes in public, Jackson built Neverland, a 2,700-acre private amusement park in California's Santa Ynez Valley.

Barbara, California, he created his own mini-Disneyworld. He named his creation Neverland.

This private amusement park features a three-story Tudor house set on 2,700 acres—more than four square miles. Armed guards patrol the grounds 24 hours a day. The ground floor of the house contains a library filled with leather-bound classics of literature. Great works of art cover the walls. A large rosewood piano dominates the living room. Huge stone fireplaces fill an entire wall of the den and the dining room. The kitchen is fully equipped, but the smell of roasting meat is never in the air, for Jackson is a vegetarian. He enjoys Mexican food but eats mostly fruit and vegetables. Down the hall is his bedroom, which looks out into a garden surrounded by a high stone wall.

On the second floor, one room is filled with dozens of dolls, and another with toys and games, coloring books and crayons, toy trucks and cars and spaceships. Life-size cutouts of Batman and the Joker and the Simpsons characters watch from the walls. A narrow stairway leads to the third-floor train room, where a complete set of Lionel trains and race-car tracks await young visitors.

Throughout the house, music is playing everywhere; but it is not just music by Michael Jackson. In addition to dance music and rock and roll, he loves to listen to classical pieces—such as *Peter and the Wolf*—ballet music, and tunes from Broadway musicals.

Outside the house, a minirailroad carries visitors past the lawns and flower beds, past a lake with boats and canoes. The oaks and sycamores abound with tuneful birds. Below them are bronze statues of young boys playing musical instruments. Hidden loudspeakers carry the sounds of music and the voices of cartoon characters.

The tracks wind past an Indian village with tepees and figures representing village life. A two-story fort is guarded by artillery that shoots streams of water. Next door, an amusement park features a carousel and Ferris wheel, bumper cars, slides, and a ride called the Zipper. The amusement park also includes a two-story building filled with electronic games and a movie theater complete with candy counter, popcorn machine, and figures of Pinocchio and E.T.

The animals in Jackson's private zoo roam about. There are horses, zebras, buffalo, ostriches, swans, deer, llamas, giraffes, and even a "zonkey" (a cross between a donkey and a zebra). Jackson's favorite animals are the monkeys and chimpanzees. His pet chimp, Bubbles, often accompanies him on trips. In 1993, Jackson obtained a license to breed rare and exotic animals. He says that he finds in animals the same thing that he finds in children—purity and honesty. "They don't judge you," he says, "they don't want anything from you, just to be your friend."

In one sense, Neverland is Jackson's attempt to compensate for all the things he missed in his childhood. Even before his fame forced him into a secluded life, he rarely enjoyed the activities that most children take for granted. "When I was little," he once told an interviewer, "it was always work, work, work from one concert to the next. If it wasn't a concert, it was the recording studio . . . TV shows or interviews or picture sessions, always something to do."

Although he rarely had time to play with other children during his own childhood, Jackson has always felt more comfortable around young people than adults. "When I was going through that bad period with my skin and my adolescent growth spurts, it was kids who never let me down," he wrote. "They were the only ones who accepted the fact that I was no longer little Michael and that I was really the same person inside, even if you didn't recognize me. I've never forgotten that. Kids are great. If I were living for no other reason than to help and please kids, that would be enough for me. They're amazing people."

Jackson's home and the grounds at Neverland are always filled with children. Young people completely take over the place when they visit. The house's third-floor train room is filled with colorful quilts for slumber parties. Michael plays with the kids and they treat him as one of them.

The grounds are always open to sick and terminally ill children, who are brought there by Jackson's Make a Wish Foundation. During a typical week, he will entertain hundreds of children with cancer. For the children who are too ill to leave their beds, Jackson has installed special hospital-style beds in the theater so they can watch cartoons, movies, and magic shows while they receive their treatment.

For a private, reclusive person, Michael Jackson suddenly seemed to be everywhere during the early months of 1993. He produced and starred in the half-time extravaganza at the Super Bowl. He appeared at two programs during the inauguration week of President Bill Clinton. He showed up on so many awards shows that he joked, "In the past month I've gone from 'Where is he?' to 'Here he is again.'" By

During the late 1980s, Michael's popularity was rivaled by the success of his younger sister, Janet. Here, the two are pictured at the 1993 Grammy Awards, where the younger Jackson presented her brother with the Grammy Living Legend Award.

the time Jackson collected his Living Legend Award at the Grammys on February 24, sales of his 1991 album *Dangerous* had zoomed from 131 on the charts to the Top 10. His latest single, "Heal the World," reached the Top 40. Both had been best-sellers overseas before taking off in the United States.

The more privacy famous people seek, the more curious the public becomes about them. In order to satisfy that curiosity, the media go to extreme lengths to try to ferret out bits and pieces of information about the object of that interest. Often, when they cannot learn the facts, they make up stories. When the celebrity remains silent and does not bother to set the record straight, the stories and rumors become accepted as truth, and the public forms a distorted view of the performer. No celebrity during the past decade has drawn more intense scrutiny than Michael Jackson.

After 14 years of silence, the 34-year-old entertainer finally agreed to do a television interview. Jackson's televised conversation with talk-show host Oprah Winfrey appeared on February 10, 1993, and was seen by more than 100 million people around the world. The two-hour program included a tour of Neverland, clips from Jackson's early performances, and the world premiere of the singer's latest video, "Give in to Me." The part of the program that drew the most attention was the actual interview. For the first time, Michael responded to the many stories and rumors that had circulated about him over the years.

During the interview, Oprah Winfrey openly confronted Jackson about some of the more outrageous rumors. One was that he slept in an oxygen chamber so he would not grow old. Jackson called the story "crazy, completely made up."

Winfrey also asked Jackson if there was any truth to the story that he campaigned to have a little white boy play his part in a Pepsi commercial. Michael said, "That's ridiculous. . . . Why would I want a white child to play me? I'm a black American. I'm proud to be a black American. . . . I have a lot of pride in who I am, and dignity."

One of the most widely published rumors about Jackson was that he had tried to bleach his skin, which had become noticeably lighter over the years. Some people speculated that he wanted to become white. Jackson vehemently denied that he had tried to whiten his skin, blaming instead a skin disorder that destroyed his skin's pigmentation. (His doctor later confirmed that Jackson suffers from vitiligo, a rare disease that discolors the skin.) "I'm trying to control it and using makeup to even it out because it makes blotches on the skin," Michael explained. He also admitted that he had twice had plastic surgery on his nose.

Jackson's close friend Elizabeth Taylor made an appearance during the interview. Taylor had also been a child star, and her understanding of what Michael had endured while growing up had established a bond between them. She described Jackson as "a wonderful, giving, caring, generous man, who is wildly funny." Jackson concluded the interview by saying that he considered himself to be an instrument of nature, chosen by God to give music and love and harmony to the world. Two of his greatest wishes were "to be known as a great artist, and to be loved wherever I go."

But there was one wish that had always motivated Michael Jackson even more. "To me, nothing is more important than making people happy," he said back in 1988, "giving them a release from their problems and worries, helping to lighten their load. I want them to walk away from a performance I've done, saying, 'That was great. I want to go back again. I had a great time.' To me, that's what it's all about."

And there is no doubt that Michael Jackson has brought such joy to millions of people. Sadly, however, in late 1993, in the midst of a world tour that saw him perform in front of millions of fans from Thailand to Mexico, came accusations that Jackson had sexually abused an adolescent boy. After months of controversy, increasingly sensational charges, and equally fervent denials, the singer agreed to pay the boy a huge settlement, which according to some reports was somewhere between $10 and $20 million. The pain and bitterness of this controversy was somewhat dispelled in May 1994, when Jackson unexpectedly announced his marriage to Lisa Marie Presley, the 26-year-old daughter of rock and roll idol Elvis Presley. Some suggested that the joining of two of pop music's most famous names was merely a publicity stunt; Jackson and Presley countered these rumors by sharing a kiss onstage during the MTV Music Awards telecast in the fall. This typically dramatic gesture suggested that Michael Jackson the man might someday enjoy the peace and happiness that Michael Jackson the entertainer has brought to so many with his music.

CHRONOLOGY

1958   Born on August 29, in Gary, Indiana

1964   The Jacksons begin to enter local talent contests

1966   The Jacksons win a citywide talent show at Roosevelt High School in Gary

1968   The Jacksons appear at the Apollo Theater in Harlem; Berry Gordy invites the Jacksons to audition for Motown Records

1969   "I Want You Back," the Jackson Five's first single with Motown, goes to #1 on charts; *Diana Ross Presents the Jackson Five* is released; immediately sells 2 million copies

1970   "ABC" hits #1 on the charts; group finishes the year with four #1 hit singles

1972   Michael's solo debut album, *Got To Be There*, released; "Ben" becomes the biggest solo Motown single of the decade

1976   The Jackson Five end their relationship with Motown; Michael, Jackie, Tito, Marlon, and Randy sign with Epic Records as The Jacksons

1977   The Jacksons perform for Queen Elizabeth II in May at Kings Hall, Glasgow, Scotland

1979   Michael releases the *Off the Wall* album, which sells 8 million copies worldwide; "Don't Stop 'Til You Get Enough" wins Grammy for Single, Best Male R & B Vocal; Michael lands role of the Scarecrow in *The Wiz*

1982   *Thriller* is released; it sells 8 million copies

1983   Michael performs on "Motown 25: Yesterday, Today, and Forever"

1984   Wins an unprecedented eight Grammy Awards for *Thriller*

1985   "We Are the World" record and video released

1986   "We Are the World" wins Grammy for Song of the Year

1988   Michael's autobiography, *Moonwalk*, published

1990   *Leave Me Alone* wins Best Music Video: Short Form, at Grammys

1991   *Dangerous* released

1993   Michael stars in the half-time extravaganza at the Super Bowl; ends 14 years of silence in live TV interview with Oprah Winfrey on February 10; receives the Living Legend Award at the Grammys

FURTHER READING

Bego, Mark. *Michael*. New York: Pinnacle Books, 1984.

George, Nelson. *The Michael Jackson Story*. New York: Dell, 1984.

Haskins, James. *About Michael Jackson*. Hillside, NJ: Enslow, 1985.

Jackson, Katherine, with Richard Wiseman. *My Family, the Jacksons*. New York: St. Martin's Press, 1990.

Jackson, Michael. *Moonwalk*. New York: Doubleday, 1988.

Latham, Caroline. *Michael Jackson Thrill*. New York: Kinsington, 1984.

Mabery, D. L. *This Is Michael Jackson*. Minneapolis: Lerner, 1994.

Marsh, Dave. *Trapped: Michael Jackson and the Crossover Dream*. New York: Bantam Books, 1985.

Pitts, Leonard. *Papa Joe's Boys: The Jackson Story*. Edited by Cindy Horner. Teaneck, NJ: Sharon, 1983.

Regan, Stewart. *Michael Jackson*. New York: Greenwich House, 1984.

Taraborrelli, Randy. *Michael Jackson: The Magic and the Madness*. New York: Ballantine Books, 1991.

INDEX

PICTURE CREDITS

———— •❦• ————

LOIS P. NICHOLSON holds a bachelor of science degree in elementary education and a master's degree in education from Salisbury State University. She has worked as a school librarian in both an elementary and a middle school in Rock Hall, Maryland. She is the author of two other biographies for Chelsea House: *George Washington Carver* (Junior World) and *Oprah Winfrey*. She has also written *Cal Ripken, Jr.: Quiet Hero* (Tidewater Publishers, 1993). Currently, she is writing a children's biography of Georgia O'Keeffe.

NATHAN IRVIN HUGGINS, one of America's leading scholars in the field of black studies, helped select the titles for the BLACK AMERICANS OF ACHIEVEMENT series, for which he also served as senior consulting editor. He was the W.E.B. Du Bois Professor of History and of Afro-American Studies at Harvard University and the director of the W.E.B. Du Bois Institute for Afro-American Research at Harvard. He received his doctorate from Harvard in 1962 and returned there as a professor in 1980 after teaching at Columbia University, the University of Massachusetts, Lake Forest College, and the California State University, Long Beach. He was the author of four books and dozens of articles, including *Black Odyssey: The Afro-American Ordeal in Slavery*, *The Harlem Renaissance*, and *Slave and Citizen: The Life of Frederick Douglass*, and was associated with the Children's Television Workshop, National Public Radio, the Boston Athenaeum, the Museum of Afro-American History, the Howard Thurman Educational Trust, and Upward Bound. Professor Huggins died in 1989, at the age of 62, in Cambridge, Massachusetts.